ENCYCLOPAEDIA OF TEACHER EDUCATION

Vol. III

INSPIRING EXPERIENCES IN TEACHER EDUCATION

By

Dr. Digumarti Bhaskara Rao

M.Sc., M.A., M.A., M.Ed., Ph.D.

Reader & Research Director

R.V.R. College of Education

Srinivasa Nagar Colony

Guntur–522 006

(India)

DISCOVERY PUBLISHING HOUSE PVT. LTD.

NEW DELHI-110 002

First Published – 2007

Reprinted – 2017

ISBN: 978-93-5056-600-8 (Set)

ISBN: 978-81-7141-656-1

Inspiring Experiences in Teacher Education

Published by:

DISCOVERY PUBLISHING HOUSE PVT. LTD.

4383/4B, Ansari Road Darya Ganj
New Delhi - 110 002 (India)
Phone: +91-11-23279245, 43596064-65
Fax: +91-11-23253475
E-mail: discoverypublishinghouse@gmail.com
sales@discoverypublishinggroup.com
web: www.discoverypublishinggroup.com

Printed at:
Infinity Imaging Systems
Delhi

DEDICATED TO

THE GREAT EDUCATIONIST

Er. Ch. V.K. Narasimha Rao
Secretary and Correspondent
Sri Prakash College of Engineering
Sri Venkateswara College of Education
SPACES Degree (UG and PG) College
Sri Prakash Residential Junior College
Sri Prakash Residential Model High School
Sri Prakash Vidya Niketan High School
Sri Prakash Nursery School
Sri Prakash Vidya Niketan
TUNI—533401
East Godavari District
Andhra Pradesh
India

Preface

The teachers play a major role in implementing the policies and schemes formulated to achieve a breakthrough in the quantitative and qualitative improvement of education. In making the teachers, many innovative experiments are in practice along with traditional teacher education programmes. This book presents some such innovative teacher education programmes which are providing inspiring experiences in teacher education and training worldwide.

The editor is thankful to UNICEF, UNESCO, International Bureau of Education, International Institute of Educational Planning, Government of India, Prof. Juan Carlos Tedesco, Rosa-Maria Torres, Amy Theobald, and UNICEF and UNESCO advisors and officials for using their articles and ideas in preparing this book for the benefit of educational personnel, teachers and teacher educators.

Bhaskara Rao Digumarti

Contents

	Preface	*v*
1.	Towards A New Paradigm of Teacher Education	1
2.	Democratic Education Workshops	17
3.	The Microcenters As a National Teacher Training Strategy	27
4.	The Training Strategy of the National Literacy Campaign "Monsignor Leonidas Proaño"	41
5.	The National In-Service Teacher Education Programme and the Community School Day Programme	62
6.	The Shiksha Karmi Project	75
7.	The Network for Teaching Upgrading Centres	83
8.	The Self-Help Action Plan for Education	109
9.	The Zimbabwe Integrated Teacher Education Course	130
10.	Early Childhood Development: More and Better: Training Trainers in the ECD Field	154
11.	The Shikshak Samakhya Project	167
12.	The Education Volunteers: New Teachers tc Take up the Challenge of Education for All	171

13. **Short-Term Teacher Training Programme** **177**

14. **Innovations and New Experiences in the Field of Teacher Education** **185**

15. **Strengthening the Role of Teachers in a Changing World** **200**

Bibliography **232**

1

Towards A New Paradigm of Teacher Education

"The Commission feels that reasserting the importance of teachers in basic education and improving teachers' qualifications are tasks to which all governments must address themselves. The measures needed to recruit future teachers from among the most motivated students, improve their training and encourage the best among them to take the most difficult posts need to be determined in relation to the specific circumstances of each country; but such measures must be taken, since, without them, it is unlikely that there will be significant improvements in quality where they are most needed. Thus, improving the quality and motivation of teachers must be a priority in all countries" (Learning: The Treasure Within, Report to UNESCO of the International Commission on Education for the Twenty-First Century, Paris, 1996: 146–147).

Background and Current Trends

Paradoxically, the global crusade to universalize basic education and improve its quality, and the proliferation of national and international commitments to accelerate the achievement of these goals by the end of the decade, have coincided with a global deterioration of teaching and of teachers' conditions. At the start of the decade (1991), the Second ILO Meeting on the Conditions of Work of Teachers concluded that the situation of teachers had reached "*an intolerably low point*", while drawing attention to the drastic erosion of teachers' working conditions worldwide and the massive exodus of qualified and experienced teachers. There is no indication that the situation has improved and, on the contrary, evidence indicates that the negative trends have been accentuated over recent years.

Teacher Education and Teacher Training

Teacher education (TE) includes both initial (or *pre-service*) and *in-service* teacher *education* and *training*. The International Standard Classification of Education (ISCED) specifies that education is "*organised and sustained communication designed to bring about learning*" in a broad sense, while the term training is reserved for "*education that is directed mainly towards the acquisition of skills*".

Teacher education (TE) has been a particularly neglected area. TE continues to be given a marginal place in education policies, generally far behind—in terms of budget allocation—school buildings and, more recently, textbooks. The overall issue—what and how do teachers learn, what do they need and want to learn, which is the best combination of modalities for TE—has not been an area of systematic research. The reforms attempted by a number of countries over the last few years have aimed at "introducing improvements" rather than at re-thinking the overall TE model.

Standards for the recruitment of basic education teachers have been lowered all over the world; at the same time, there is a tendency to reduce the time allocated to both *initial* and *in-service* TE. In other words: teachers with less (or poor) general education themselves are being trained not in more but in less time. This is clearly contradictory to the declared objective of improving the quality of basic education.

The traditional subordination of teacher-related issues has been reinforced in recent times by cost-reduction policies as well as by a number of studies which conclude that teacher knowledge and salaries have little impact on student learning outcomes, as compared with inputs such as libraries, time of instruction, homework, and textbooks. Against this perception, teacher *education* tends to be reduced to narrow teacher *training* approaches, and efforts are concentrated in short *in-service* (to the detriment of *pre-service*) TE. Teacher education continues to be viewed in isolation, disconnected from other factors that shape the role and performance of teachers (recruitment, salary, work conditions, and overall professional development).

Education reform processes tend to maintain the classical scheme of incorporating teachers when the proposal has already been defined, counting on teachers only as potential trainees and implementors, thus disregarding the importance of teachers' knowledge, experience and active participation in the reform process. The common approach of adapting teachers to the reform proposal, rather than adapting the reform proposal to teachers, is still dominant.

Fortunately, there are also positive trends and innovative experiences emerging in various countries. In general, however, such initiatives are recent are still limited in size, and more often linked to *in-service* rather than to *pre-service* TE.

Delineating a Strategy for Teacher Education Efforts

- ***Closing the Gap Between Educational Objectives and Teacher Competencies:*** Achieving education for all and improving the quality of education implies a substantial improvement in the professional status and quality of teachers. The building of the "new education" and the "new teacher role" by the 21st Century calls for integral and urgent measures directed towards reversing the present profile and situation of teachers in all spheres. Failing which, the goals set for the end of the century and beyond will remain unachievable.

- ***Teachers as Learners:*** The modern education slogan of "*focusing on learning*" underscored by the World Conference on Education for All (Jomtien, Thailand, 1990), needs to be understood as a vindication not only of students but of teachers themselves. Ensuring and improving student learning in school implies, as a prerequisite, ensuring teachers the opportunities and conditions for relevant, permanent and qualitative learning in order for them to be able to face their new expected roles.

- ***Teacher Education as a Continuum:*** Pre-and in-service TE must be viewed as part of one single process, thus revindicating the concept and principles of *continuing education* for the teaching profession. The long-acknowledged need to articulate the various levels of the education system (pre-school, primary, secondary, tertiary) requires changes not only in the administration and the curriculum but, most importantly, in TE so as to favour coherence and continuity between such levels.

- ***Reviewing Cost-effectiveness Criteria Applied to Teacher Education:*** The relationship between teacher knowledge (and TE) and student learning outcomes is not a mechanical one. Many of the factors that intervene in student learning are beyond the control of teachers and exceed their professional knowledge or competence. Teachers' roles and actual performance have an impact that goes beyond academic achievement as measured by school tests and grades. Moreover, as demonstrated by several studies, teachers' attitudes and expectations (not necessarily attributable to their professional training) can be more determinant in student learning than their mastery of the subject or of pedagogy. All this implies reviewing narrow cost-effectiveness criteria applied to TE.

- ***Technical and Technological Solutions are Not the Priority:*** It is necessary to create the political, cultural, information—and knowledge-related conditions that are essential to promote changes in societal perceptions and attitudes towards teachers and their work, so that governments, teachers associations, societies and international organisations involved in the education sector acknowledge—not only in rhetoric but in practice-the important role of teachers and the need to improve their working and professional conditions as a fundamental step towards quality education for all. Teacher associations are, of course, expected to be the leading forces in this initiative, but in order to be effective they must review their own traditional agendas and negotiating methods, incorporating TE as an important contributor to professional identity and development.

- ***School Autonomy Implies Teacher Autonomy:*** Within the current education decentralization thrust, continuous references are made to *school autonomy* and *teacher autonomy*. It is important, however, to bear in mind that school autonomy can take place without *teacher* autonomy (for example, decentralization or deconcentration of administrative or financial management, while the status and role of teachers remain unchanged). *Teacher autonomy* implies, essentially, *professional autonomy*, and this requires specific measures. Promoting greater school autonomy without creating the conditions for greater professional autonomy for teachers may contribute to strengthen, rather than to alleviate, inefficiency, inequity and poor quality in education systems.

- ***An Integral Approach to Teacher Professional Development:*** It is not possible to isolate TE from the remaining factors that influence teacher performance and development. Professional quality is inseparable from quality of life. In the context of the current low economic, moral and professional incentives offered to teachers today, access to higher levels of knowledge and training often (and foreseeably) leads to better job alternatives. The difficulty in attracting the best candidates and in retaining qualified and experienced teachers results in a high rotation of personnel and a continuous starting point for TE efforts around the world. All of which indicate the obvious: TE must be viewed as part of an integral package of measures aimed at enhancing the teaching profession, and implemented within the framework of substantial changes in the organisation and culture of the school system as a whole.

Rethinking Teacher Education

"*The Commission believes that a rethinking of teacher education is necessary, in order for it to bring out in future teachers precisely those human and intellectual qualities that will facilitate a fresh approach to teaching*" (Learning: The Treasure Within, Report to UNESCO of the International Commission on Education for the Twenty-First Century, Paris 1996: 146).

The profound changes required for TE call not for more of the same—more time, more subjects, more courses—but rather for a transformation of the conventional TE model which has displayed its inefficiency and ineffectiveness in meeting the needs of teachers and their advancement, and of students and their improved learning processes and results (see box).

The new paradigm of TE must take into account issues such as the following:

- Introducing changes in the general education (school system) of future teachers.
- Ensuring acceptable working and remuneration conditions, so as to make teaching an attractive option and TE a cost-effective investment.
- Defining new policies and criteria for the selection and recruitment of new teachers.
- Redefining teachers' roles within the framework of the necessary redefinition of the role of the school system and of education.
- Building a unified TE system that views pre-service and in-service learning as a continuum.
- Rethinking the organisational and administrative modalities for TE.
- Redefining priorities in the allocation of resources within the education sector.

THE TEACHER EDUCATION MODEL THAT HAS NOT WORKED

• each new policy, plan or project starts from zero	(ignoring or disregarding previous knowledge and experience)
• considers education/training principally as a need for teachers	(and not also for principals, supervisors and human resources linked to the education system in general and at all levels)
• views education/training in isolation from other dimensions of the teaching profession	(such as salaries, working and living conditions, promotion mechanisms, organisational arrangements, etc.)
• ignores teachers' real conditions	(motivations, concerns, knowledge, available time and resources. etc.)
• adopts a top-down approach and sees teachers only in a passive role of recipients and potential trainees	(does not consult teachers or seek their participation in the definition and design of the training plan)
• has a homogeneous proposal for "teachers" in general	(instead of adjusting to the various types and levels of teachers and their specific needs)
• adopts an operational approach to teacher training	(in-service training is viewed as a tool to persuade and implement a definite policy, programme, project or even a textbook)

(Contd...)

• assumes that the need for training is inversely proportional to the level of teaching	(thus ignoring the importance and complexity of teaching young children and in the initial grades)
• resorts to external incentives and motivation mechanisms	(such as scores, promotion, certificates, rather than reinforcing the objective of learning and improving the teaching practice)
• addresses individual teachers	(rather than groups or work teams, or the school as a unified whole)
• is conducted outside the work place	(typically, teachers are brought to the training sites instead of bringing the training to them and making the school the training site)
• is a systematic and limited to a short period of time	(not integral to a continuing education scheme)
• is centred around the event (the course, the seminar, the workshop, etc.) as a privileged-and even unique—teaching and learning tool visits, etc.)	(ignoring or marginalizing other modalities such as horizontal exchange, peer group discussions, class observation, distance education, self-study, on-site)
• disassociates administrative and pedagogical issues as content and as learning needs	(pedagogical issues are considered the realm of teachers, and administrative issues are consigned to others, without an integral approach to both types of knowledge and skills)

• disassociates content and method (subject matter and pedagogy, knowing the subject and knowing how to teach it) and promotes the prior over the latter	(ignoring the inseparability and complementarity of both types of knowledge, and the need for both)
• considers education and training to be formal, stem and rigid	(denying the educational and communicational importance of an informal environment, of play, laughter and enjoyment)
• is focused on the teaching perspective	(rather than on the learning perspective)
• rejects teachers' previous knowledge and experience	(instead of starting from there and building on it)
• is oriented towards correcting mistakes and highlighting weaknesses	(rather than at stimulating and reinforcing strengths)
• is academic and theoretical, centred around the book	(while denying the actual teaching practice as the raw material and the most important source for learning)
• is based on the frontal and transmissive teaching model	(teaching as the transmission of information and learning as the passive assimilation of that information)
• is essentially incohesive and contradictory to the pedagogical model that is requested of teachers in their classrooms	(teachers are expected to elicit active learning critical thinking, creativity, etc., which they themselves do not experience in their own education and training process)

- Renovating the TE curriculum (objectives, content, approaches, methods, strategies, techniques, resources, means).
- Taking into account the rhythms and time frames that are required to break away from the vicious circle, to advance while showing results, and to create conditions for sustainability.
- Setting up a coordinated and systematic information, communication and public opinion effort aimed at the social revaluation of teachers and of the teaching profession.
- Reviewing the conventional relationship and dialogue between the State, civil society and teacher associations.

Where? Sources of Teacher Learning

Teacher learning generally evokes teacher *training* and the latter is generally divided into *pre-service* and *in-service*. However, what teachers learn (or may learn) in a systematic manner derives from various sources: the school *system* (teachers are ex-students), the specialized *TE programme* (whether pre-or in-service), and the teaching *practice*. Empirical evidence suggests that teachers tend to replicate whatever they learned (as part of the "hidden" school curriculum) about teaching and learning when they were school students. Reforming the school system must thus be viewed as a critical intervention to improve TE and teacher performance. Also, self-reflection and systematization of their own pedagogical practice is the best tool teachers have for their professional advancement.

Accepting the existence of various teacher learning sources and environments implies accepting the existence of, and the need for, *diverse modalities of* TE.

How? Strategies and Modalities for Teacher Learning

Teacher Education as a Strategy

The preparation and upgrading of human resources in any field requires a long-term and sustained effort. This implies adopting a *strategic* vision in the field of TE, and designing TE as a *strategy* in itself. The lack of strategic vision and strategy has nurtured the classical dichotomic options: *pre*-versus *in-service* TE, *subject (general)* versus *pedagogical (specialized)* knowledge, *theory* versus *practice, residential (face-to-face)* versus *distance* education modalities, etc. If we consider TE a continuous process, realized through various sources and developed through different stages, we are faced not with options but rather with priorities, and with the need to select the most appropriate combinations and sequences: Where to start? How to continue? When and how to introduce the various topics and goals? How to combine theory and practice? What should be included in pre-service TE and what is better learned—or can only be learned—concurrent with the teaching practice? What requires face-to-face interaction and what can be done with distance education? How and when to introduce self-instructional modalities?

Some elements to consider when defining a TE strategy are:

- Teacher *education* is more than teacher *training*. Meeting the complex demands posed on teachers today requires a broad teacher *education* effort (understanding of the phenomena and problems, and development of theoretical-practical competencies to identify and solve them) which necessarily involves a *training* dimension (development of skills necessary to accomplish specific tasks).
- *Starting* from teacher needs and demands, in order to build up on them.
- Promoting teacher-to-teacher approaches and collegial work, thus breaking with the traditional isolation of teaching.
- *Widening* and diversifying TE teaching modalities, searching for the combination of modalities best suited for each particular circumstance and context. *Face-to-face* and *distance* teaching are not opposing categories: face-to-face contact and feedback are essential in good distance teaching.
- "Seeing" change in action, by facilitating teachers with an opportunity for exposure (visits, readings, etc.) to innovative programmes, exemplary practices, demonstrative schools, etc.

- Viewing teacher education as *adult* education, thus incorporating valuable knowledge and practical experience accumulated within the adult education field.
- Incorporating pedagogical practice as a permanent source of teacher systematic reflection, analysing and learning.
- Encouraging self-study and self-learning.
- Acknowledging the importance of play and fun in teachers' learning processes and experiences.

> In as much as TE is, by definition, adult education, the linkages between both areas seem obvious and fruitful. In Latin America, bridges are being built between the adult education movement—and the *Popular Education* movement, in particular—and the formal school system, often with an active role in TE.
>
> Play, laughter, music, dance, should constitute any TE programme, particularly for teachers involved with children's education. Part of the secret of the *Shikshak Samakhya* ("Teacher Empowerment") programme in Madhya Pradesh, India, is described in terms of teachers experiencing "*an explosion of ideas, knowledge, skills and interactive activities, a wide range of colourfoul and attractive teaching learning materials, different methods of teaching, collegiality and peer group support*"

What? Teachers' Basic Learning Needs

"*Teachers must adapt their relationship with learners, switching roles from 'soloist' to 'accompanist', and shifting the emphasis from dispensing information to helping learners seek, organise and manage knowledge, guiding them rather than molding them*" (Learning: The Treasure Within, Report to UNESCO of the International Commission on Education for the Twenty-First Century, Paris 1996: 144).

From the perspective of the TE curriculum, the critical question that needs to be addressed is: what are teachers' *basic learning needs* (knowledge, skills, values and attitudes) in order to cope with the new profile and role demanded from them? In other words, what do teachers need to learn to become *learning facilitators, flexible orientators, habitual readers, curriculum developers, reflective researchers in the classroom, community promoters and organisers, systematizers of their own experience, active members of a study group, critical intellectuals, autonomous professionals*?

Some basic principles appear to be important in responding to these questions:

- Incorporating teachers as active participants in the definition of their own learning needs.
- Harmonizing the school curriculum with the TE curriculum.
- Ensuring an adequate combination of both *general* (subject) and *specialized* (pedagogical) knowledge, covering the various areas of teacher competence.
- Including not only cognitive but also attitudinal and emotional aspects within the TE curriculum. Love, affection, understanding, care, sensitivity and respect for students and their differences, are part of the quality of education and of the quality of a teacher.
- Diversifying the TE curriculum in accordance with varied needs of teachers.
- Prioritizing the gaps in the basic education of teachers (basic knowledge, skills, values and attitudes).
- Taking nothing for granted: It has been customary to place demands on teacher competencies that are taken for granted and, as such, are not (or are only formally) included in TE, such as the capacity to innovate; organising (or participating in) group work; designing and administering homework; adapting the curriculum; test design; evaluation of student learning achievement; promoting parental and community participation; organising play and "extra-curricular" activities. All these require and involve specialized knowledge and skills that can be learned.
- Prioritizing certain problem-areas of school performance such as the teaching and learning of reading and writing, a critical factor in school success or failure; repetition, its factors and

consequences; time of instruction and its relationship with student learning; multigrade systems; proper and timely identification of "*learning* difficulties" (as opposed to "*teaching* difficulties").

AREAS OF TEACHER COMPETENCE

1. teaching, for what?	education objectives and goals; learning as the ultimate purpose of teaching
2. whom to teach?	getting to know the students, their family, cultural and social background
3. where to teach?	the classroom, the school institution, the teaching-learning environment, the community
4. what to teach?	curriculum content: knowledge, skills, values and attitudes
5. how to teach?	pedagogical competencies in general, and for each subject or area in particular
6. with what to teach?	means and materials for teaching
7. what and how to evaluate?	competencies to evaluate both teaching and learning
8. how to improve teaching and learning?	competencies to continuously improve practice (observation, self-reflection, self-study, research, systematization, exchange, group work, etc.)

REFERENCES

Arancibia, V. 1988. "Didáctica de la educación primaria", in C. Muñoz Izquierdo (ed.), *Calidad equidad y eficiencia de la educación primaria: estado actual de las investigaciones realizadas en América Latina,* CEE-REDUC, Mexico.

Avalos, B.; Haddad, W. 1981. *A Review of Teacher Effectiveness Research in Africa, India, Latin America, Middle East, Malaysia, Philippines and Thailand: Synthesis of Results,* IDRC, Ottawa.

Avalos, B. 1991. *Approaches to Teacher Education: Initial Teacher Training.* Commonwealth Secretariat, London.

Condevin, G.; Naidu, S. 1989. "In-service Education at a Distance: Trends in Third World Development", in *Opening Learning.*

Cox, C. 1989. "La formación del profesorado: saber e instituciones", in: Garcia-Huidobro, J.E. (ed.) *Escuela, calidad e igualdad: Los desafíos para educar en democracia,* CIDAE, Santiago.

Dyer, C. 1996. "Primary Teachers and Policy Innovation in India", in *DPEP Calling,* Issue N° 15, New Delhi.

Ezpeleta, J; Furlán, A. (comp.) 1992. *La gestión pedagógica de la escuela,* UNESCO-OREALC, Santiago.

Flip, J.; Cardemil, C.; Valdivieso, C. 1984. *Profesoras y profesores efectivos en Chile,* CIDE, Santiago.

Gallén, V; Bold, J. 1989. *Saskatchewan Teachers' Federation Study on Teaching Saskatchewan* Teachers' Federation, Saskatoon.

Gimeno Sacristán, J. 1992. "Investigación e innovacion sobre la gestión pedagógica de los equipos de profesores", in *La gestión pedagógica de la escuela,* UNESCO-OREALC, Santiago.

Hallak, J. 1990. *Investing in the Future: Setting Educational Priorities in the Developing World,* IIEP-UNESCO, Paris.

Heneveld, W.; Criag, H. 1995. "Effective Schools: Determining Which Factors Have the Greatest Impact", in *DAE Newsletter,* Vol. 7, N° 3, Paris, July-Septembe..

Heyneman, S.P. 1995. "Economic of Education: Disappointments and Potential", in *Prospects,* Vol. XXV, N° 4, UNESCO-IBE, Geneva.

Klees, S.J. 1994. "The Economics of Educational Technology", in T. Husen and T. Neville Postlethwaite (eds.), in *The International Encyclopedia of Education* (2a. edition), Pergamon, Oxford.

Perraton. H. 1994. *Alternative Routes to Formal Education: Distance Teaching for School Equivalency*, A World Bank Research Publication, The Johns Hopkins University Press, London/Baltimore.

Schiefelbein, E.; Braslavsky, C.; Gatti, B.; Farrés, P. 1994. "Las características de la profesión maestro y la calidad de la educación en América Latina", in *Boletín del Proyecto Principal en América Latina y el Caribe*, N° 34, UNESCO-OREALC, Santiago.

Torres, R.M. 1993. "¿Qué (y cómo) es necesario aprender? *Necesidades básicas de aprendizaje y contenidos curriculares básicas de aprendizaje: Estrategias de acción*, UNESCO-OREALC/IDRC, Santiago.

Torres, R.M. 1996. "Teacher Education: From Rhetoric to Action", in UNESCO-ACEID/UNICEF, *Partnerships in Teacher Development for a New Asia*, Bangkok.

Torres, R.M. 1996. "Improving Basic Education? World Bank Strategies", in N. Stromquist (ed.), *Politics of Educational Innovations in Developing Nations: An Analysis of Knowledge and Power*, Garland Publishing, New York (forthcoming).

UNESCO. 1991. *World Education Report*, Paris.

UNESCO. 1996. *Learning: The Treasure Within*, Report to UNESCO of the International Commission on Education for the Twenty-First Century, Paris.

UNICEF-ROSA. 1996. *The SAFDED Workshop on Distance Education Initiatives in Teacher Education in South Asia with Focus on Primary and Secondary Levels*, ROSA Report N° 8, Kathmandu.

Vera, R. 1985. "Talleres de educadores. Una línea de perfeccionamiento docente", in *Dialogando*, N° 10, Santiago.

WORLD BANK. 1995. *Priorities and Strategies for Education: A World Bank Review*, Washington D.C.

Rosa-Maria Torres
Senior Education Advisor
UNICEF Education Cluster
New York USA.

Courtesy: UNICEF & UNESCO,
EFA: Making it Work.

2

Democratic Education Workshops

In Chile, as in most of Latin America, the main challenge currently facing school systems lies in improving the equity and quality of the education. This implies a focus on teaching-learning processes in the classroom and in the quality of such processes. In turn, this requires placing teachers and teacher education and upgrading central to all reform efforts.

Since educational change requires the active participation of teachers, and since teachers must at the same time be promoters of change and subjects of change themselves, teachers organisations must assume a leading role in promoting teacher professionalization and upgrading. The long history and strong presence of teacher unions in many Latin American countries place these in a key position for large-scale involvement of teachers in the process of change and self-change.

These were some of the basic premises that led to the creation of the *Talleres de Educación Democrática*—TED (Democratic Education Workshops). TED started in 1987 as a joint initiative of the World Confederation of Professional Teacher Associations (CMOPE); the *Programa Interdisciplinario de Investigaciones en Educación*—Interdisciplinary Programme for Educational Research (PIIE), a Chilean

NGO; and the Teacher Federation of Norway. TED emerged as a proposal for teacher empowerment to be owned and conducted by teacher professional associations.

TED was initiated in Chile and later expanded to other Latin American countries. It was implemented in agreement with teacher unions in Chile (*Colegio de Profesores*), Peru (*Sindicato Unico de Trabajadores*—SUTEP), and Paraguay (*Organización de Trabajadores de la Educación de Paraguay*—OTEP). The programme lasted seven years and formally concluded in December 1993.

TED's Objectives and Methodology

TED operated through workshops where teachers met to reflect upon and evaluate their professional experience, in order to rethink their role as educators and to transform their pedagogical practice into a more efficient and democratic one. Teachers met with a common desire to develop and improve their teaching practice, as well as to share and evaluate the innovations that they were defining and experimenting with. TED's overall aim was contributing to transforming teacher organisations from within, and to propell them towards undertaking a lead role in school reform and entering the social debate on education and education policies. TED worked towards generating a renovated pedagogical movement within teacher organisations from which bottom-up and school-centred reform proposals could arise.

The underlying principle was that "*teachers will be able to consciously and creatively modify their teaching practice in as much as they are able to acquire the capacity to analyze it critically*" (Vera, 1985). In other words, placing teachers in contact with new educational theories or teaching methods and techniques, or providing schools with modern educational technology, may be of little value and have little impact on changing teacher practices and improving teaching in the classroom unless teachers and convinced of the need to change. This can only occur through a process of personal awareness. Teachers thus need to be assisted with the necessary knowledge and conditions to take an objective look at their practice, reflect on it critically, compare it with that or other colleagues, identify and understand the problems they face, and value their own knowledge, experience and creativity.

LEARNING OBJECTIVES OF TED

TED workshops aimed at modifying the internal world of the educator in ways that would enable him or her to break with some of the main problems of the traditional school culture: authoritarianism, dogmatism, bureaucracy and technocratism. To accomplish this, TED had three learning objectives:

(a) changing the educator's role: from a merely *technical* role to a *professional* role;

(b) changing teachers' working practice: from *isolated* work to *collective* work; and

(c) changing the modes of teacher's learning: from *dependent* learning to *autonomous* learning.

Changing the Educator's Role: From a *Technical* Role to a *Professional* Role

The role of the teacher as a "technician" is externally programmed. Everything—the content of teaching, the methods and pace of teaching, the exercises to use in the class and the modalities of evaluation—are provided for the teacher. Teachers are alienated from their work, do not understand the *whys, hows,* and *what fors* of what they do on a daily basis. They have no say in the decisions that shape the teaching profession and role. Professional autonomy and professional responsibility are interrelated. The teacher who accepts being reduced to an implementor of curricula and textbooks abandons the possibility of understanding the complexity of teaching and of learning, and only demands ready-made formulas from teacher training courses and programmes. Teaching thus becomes a mechanical and repetitive task, devoid of the pleasure of teaching, and often therefore denying such pleasure to students in their own learning.

The professional teacher, on the other hand, is more capable of diagnosing complex situations, of understanding that students confront diverse types of difficulties in the process of learning, have different learning styles, and therefore require different teaching styles that respect their group and individual learning needs, interests and experiences. The professional teacher is more proactive, takes greater initiative, is more flexible, has original ideas, is more creative, and has a wider global vision. He/she asserts more control over the act of teaching.

To achieve this objective, TED workshops aimed at creating conditions for teachers to modify the relationship they have with their work, which in turn implies modifying the way teachers perceive themselves and their role as educators.

Changing Teachers' Working Practice: From *Isolated* Work to *Collective* Work

The technocratic organisational structure of schools makes it difficult for teachers to project teaching as a professional competence, and bureaucratic structures in schools pre-suppose teaching as an individual, isolated, lonely task.

Teachers in the same school may not have any contact with each other or systematically share the teaching and learning problems they face. They resist confronting experiences together. They are afraid to be evaluated and therefore afraid to evaluate others. Competitiveness among teachers is far more common than cooperation.

TED workshops tried to create adequate conditions for educators to change the ways in which they approach their work and to be more cooperative. Therefore, there was a strong emphasis on group work.

Changing the Modes of Teachers' Learning: From *Dependent* to *Autonomous* Learning

Just as teachers have internalized competitiveness instead of cooperative relationships, they have internalized dependent forms of learning.

The school system traditionally favours authoritarian relations between teachers and students, and a dogmatic approach to the curriculum and to pedagogy. Teachers prefer their students to repeat information rather than to think, ask or argue; to copy from books rather than to conduct research based in reality; or to respond with what the teacher wants to hear rather than to let students incorporate their own experiences. Through this process, student learning ends up depending almost totally on teacher teaching.

Developing an education system that is based on and enhances autonomous learning, where learners recount their own experiences and then reflect on and convert these experiences into knowledge, requires a major shift in school systems and in the overall conceptualization of education.

In order to foster an understanding of the process of autonomous learning vis a vis dependent learning, TED workshops aimed at creating adequate conditions for the participants to convert workshop experiences into teaching material. By learning to be autonomous learners teachers are better able to accept that their students are autonomous learners themselves.

TED LEARNING CONDITIONS

TED methodology was based on three elements:

(a) teacher research on their pedagogical practice;

(b) group work; and

(c) on-going evaluation of teacher learning.

Teacher Research: Learning to Reflect Critically on One's Own Practice

A redefinition of teachers' role requires teachers to assume a critical perspective on their role so as to perceive the difference between authoritarian and democratic teaching, and between dependent and autonomous learning. Teachers must distance themselves from their work in order to understand how they internalized their conventional roles, how they become comfortable in those assigned roles, and how such roles are translated in their pedagogical practice. Only then can teachers begin to assume an alternative role. TED offered teachers the possibility of trying their new role within the workshop before they could exercise it in the classroom.

The Research Workshop thus provided an important environment for teachers to engage in critical self-evaluation, analyze and discuss the problems they face in their schools and classrooms, and generate knowledge on how to address those problems in an alternative manner.

Research conducted at the workshops dealt with daily problems at schools such as the exercising of discipline, lack of motivation of students, pace of teaching and learning, heterogeneous groups, lack of parental interest, and institutional conflicts.

Although a research method was recommended and followed, such research did not aspire to validate knowledge. It assisted the participants in raising issues of concern, posing questions, thinking and arguing more rigorously, and developing a better understanding of the issues discussed. Research started from practice and from a critical analysis of such practice, and valued teacher knowledge, common sense and experience.

Group Work: Learning to Work Collaboratively

Since one of the objectives of TED was changing the teachers' work style from isolated to cooperative, workshops utilized a group methodology that helped teachers experienced what they are required to do in their classrooms and in their professional relationships with colleagues.

A cooperative group has democratic relationships. It enables participants to combine solidarity and liberty, equity and diversity, individual identities and group interest. The cooperative group is an effective strategy for learning, research and action. The feeling of group work is shared, and individuals use their energies towards the task at hand, each contributing to the social dynamic and to its expected outcomes.

Evaluation: Learning to Learn

At the end of each workshop, participants reflected upon what they had experienced, the method used, and the ways through which they interacted in their work or when facing resistance within the group. The evaluation served as a way for teachers to learn how to learn from their experiences.

FRAMEWORK OF THE WORKSHOPS

Certain conditions are essential for a group to work effectively. TED termed these conditions a "framework" that includes space, time and roles.

Each workshop had three phases:

(a) information;

(b) group work; and

(c) evaluation.

Phase I: Information

The first step is an informative one. The objective is to gather teachers' knowledge and input on the topic being researched. This encourages the expression of common sense, ordinary knowledge, concerns, fears, and expectations. Listening to each other is the main activity.

Phase II: Group Work

During this phase of the workshop, the participants work in groups and conduct the research in four stages:

1. *Defining the problem* through four steps:

   (a) Participants share conflict situations experienced in the classroom or at school: an incident with a student or a group of students, a colleague, an administrator, or parents.

   (b) After each teacher shares an experience, the group discusses and decides which one should be analyzed. The process of

coming to consensus makes the participants explain and defend their choices. Finally, the group makes a consensual, democratic decision.

(c) From the event selected, the group defines the problem to be studied (e.g. the conduct of the teacher in the incident chosen).

(d) The group converts the problem into a research project (e.g. developing questions to try to understand the teacher's conduct in that particular situation).

2. *Objectifying the problem* The group reconstructs the incident extremely and internally, distancing themselves from the situation in order to objectify the problem. This can be done through

   (a) ***External Reconstruction:*** the teacher was lived through the incident describes it from a new perspective—as an observer instead of the protagonist. Other group members assist the teacher by asking questions, but without value judgements.

   (b) ***Internal Reconstruction:*** the teacher involved in the incident describes it from his/her own perspective. He/she describes the emotions felt at the time, the reasons why he/she thinks the other protagonists acted the way they did, and rationalizes the action taken. Other group members assist by asking questions.

3. *Interpretation of the problem* Group members interpret the incident. First, they discuss the psycho-socio-pedagogical and institutional conceptions that are revealed by the incident. They ask questions, discuss, and develop hypotheses as to why the situation occurred. Then, they try to relate the incident to the larger institutional environment.

4. *Development of alternatives* Teachers formulate alternative actions for the incident that was analyzed, based on the group discussions, and using dramatization, brain-storming and other techniques. They then discuss what changes should be introduced within the school system and culture in order to institute the alternative proposals.

The TED coordinator cooperates with the groups so that they assume their role of being collective, democratic and responsible. In this way, the coordinator operates from outside the group, concentrating on the group structure, observing the group, but not engaging him/herself in their research project. The coordinator does not define the work nor orient the participants on the steps to follow to accomplish the task. He/she intervenes only to tell workshop members his/her perception of the group's process and of the obstacles they face.

Phase III: Evaluation

The evaluation is a time of introspection for each participant to reflect on what was learned during the first two phases and on how that will assist him/her in confronting similar situations in the future.

The fundamental objective of this evaluative phase is to stimulate participants to continue learning for themselves through the process that was experienced with the group during the workshop. The aim is to instill a permanent attitude towards reflection that goes beyond the workshops.

TED operated in Chile, Colombia, Paraguay and Peru. In all these countries, teacher associations supported TED, facilitated an environment receptive to change by those who participated in the workshops, and prepared training cadres within each teacher association so as to strengthen its educational and pedagogical work and ensure the continuation of the effort. These trainers were trained as TED workshop coordinators thus multiplying, within each teacher association, the capacity for conducting their own workshops. By 1992, in Chile, over 600 teachers had participated in TED, 120 of whom become TED workshop coordinators. In Peru workshops reached more than 200 teachers in Lima and in the Chavin Region. Fifteen of these were trained as workshop coordinators; they coordinate workshops and assist the Department of Pedagogical Affairs of SUTEP. In Paraguay, approximately 100 teachers and 15 workshop coordinators were trained in Asunción and some of the interior provinces.

TED planted the seed to interest teacher associations and unions in pedagogical reflection and advancement within their organisations. In addition to the workshops and diverse initiatives taken by workshop leaders, TED led to the formation of groups of teachers who, with varying degrees of regularity, meet to consider daily pedagogic practices, to study, and to propose alternatives to problems in education. Members of these groups feel part of a growing educational movement. The transformation and building process initiated by TED thus continues, even though the programme ended in December 1993.

Sources

- Jenny Assael, Talleres de Educación Democrática (TED), *Cómo aprende y cómo enseña el docente: Informe de Seminario,* PIIE/ICI, Santiago, 1992.
- Rodrigo Vera, "Talleres de educadores. Una línea de perfeccionamiento participativo", in: *Dialogando*, N° 10, Santiago, 1985.
- *Momento Informativo*, Boletín N° 20, Santiago, December 1993.
- Talleres de Educación Democrática TED, Santiago, 1990.

—Rosa-Maria Torres UNICEF
Courtesy: UNICEF-UNESCO,
Education For All: Making It Work

3

The Microcenters As a National Teacher Training Strategy

The expansion of the Curricular Renewal (*Renovación Curricular*) movement throughout the country (Decree 1002 of 1984), and a recognition of the difficulties faced by traditional approaches to teacher training, led the Colombian Ministry of Education (MEN) to experiment with alternative strategies for teacher education. It was officially stated that "*teacher training must be related to improvements in the quality and efficiency of education and of the national school system. This means that training must be targeted to preventing school failure, while enhancing the teacher as an individual, as a professional and as promoter of development*"..

Several studies conducted in Colombia have described the predominant pedagogical practice as rote learning, repetitive, authoritarian, discipline-centered, obedience-oriented, individualistic, and non-critical. A wide gap persists between pedagogical theory, teacher education and teaching practice. Traditionally, *in-service training* had been centered around courses and tied to bureaucratic regulations, with little connection to reality and to teachers' needs and practice.

Against this context, the MEN decided to revise the concept of teacher education, its objectives, approaches and modalities, particularly for in-service training. It was acknowledged that further training must help teachers fulfil their role as teachers as well as promoters of the community and social development, a role that requires teachers to possess theoretical and practical teaching competencies; be informed about, and have an opportunity to discuss, national education policies; have a deep understanding of the community and the environment where they work; and develop a high degree of social responsibility.

From this analysis emerged the Microcentros (Microcenters) for urban areas, and the *Escuela Demostrativa* (Demonstration School) for the rural areas. The Microcenter was defined as "*the basic cell of educational organisation at the municipal level which consists of forming working groups of teachers and/or headmasters from one or several educational institutions at pre-school, primary, junior secondary and vocational secondary levels in order to carry out teacher-to-teacher training activities aimed at identifying needs, analyzing them, and searching for the best solution so that the problem can be resolved within the classroom, the educational institution, and the community*".

> "*Despite difficulties, achievements have been obtained with the work at the Microcenters. One of these has been a questioning of traditional pedagogical practices. Another is new approaches to learning issues. Lastly, a new strategy for teacher training. There are already several teachers who have begun go develop small education research projects that fit the needs of the environment. For instance, a group of teachers has been working on the history of their municipality through a participatory methodology. Others work on new methodologies for the development of joyful learning and artistic activities. Difficulties still confront us, but if a better comprehension of the real function of teachers is achieved, the Microcenters may significantly have played a role in the development of a new cultural project.*" (Director of CEID, El Huila section).

The Microcenter was thus conceived as an on-the-spot in-service teacher training strategy that would offer teachers an opportunity to engage in a teacher-to-teacher education process in which concepts are built, experiences are shared and solutions are envisioned and applied by teachers in their daily work. Thus, the Microcenter strategy implied deep changes not only in teachers' attitude but in the overall school culture.

A number of organisational and administrative conditions were foreseen to enable teacher groups to meet and benefit from counselling, tutoring and permanent feedback from technical teams at the local and regional level. With this purpose, the MEN published basic guidelines for the organisation, functioning and assistanship of the Microcenters in a series of *Bulletins*. Later, working methodologies were defined for the teacher-to-teacher exchange and to ensure that the overall Microcenter strategy had an impact on the quality of education and on increased teachers' awareness of their social responsibility.

> "*If we, teachers, do not reflect on what we do, we mechanize ourselves and we are not going to be aware of the problems and difficulties we have to overcome. The Microcenter is a tool that helps to detect conflicting points and possibilities for transforming the school*".

Work at the Microcenters is structured around two elements:

(a) the *Pedagogical Workshop* aims at finding concrete answers to the problems faced by teachers in their handling of the curriculum and their relationship with parents.

Such problems are discussed through group work, experience exchange and individual inputs; and

(b) the *Educational Project*, defined as "*the sequence of planned tasks with a practical aim that should be attained by means of co-operative work*".

Microcenters are now widespread in the country and viewed as a key strategy within the overall movement towards the improvement of Colombian education. In order to link teachers and their experiences at a national scale, an annual workshop called *Productos* (Products) enables teachers from different regions to demonstrate and discuss their initiatives and innovations.

"Traditional teacher training is based on a vertical advisor-student-teacher relationship, a simple, mechanical teaching-learning process that corresponds to the dictates of behaviourism. At the Microcenters it is possible to implement a new type of in-service training, where the relationship becomes horizontal, experiences are shared, and both the advisor [orientador] and the teacher teach and learn".

"Since [in the conventional in-service teacher training scheme] it is mandatory to obtain credits to receive a promotion, the teacher will not pay attention to the course that best improves his or her work. Instead teachers will take the first one they find even if it is useless to them. The important thing is to take the course and obtain the credit. The result is that what we get will never be applied, it is something that always remains up in the air"

MICROCENTERS AT WORK: THE RESULTS OF A STUDY

Research in the field of teacher education has been neglected in Colombia and other Latin American countries. Aware of this, the *Universidad Pedagógica Nacional* (National Pedagogic University) undertook research in this area. Such research has contributed to bring to the surface the crisis of teacher education in the country, particularly of in-service teacher training, and to promote experimentation with alternative strategies. Against this background, an exploratory study was undertaken in the Department of El Huila to assess the performance of local Microcenters.

The study, covering quantitative and qualitative dimensions, aimed at analyzing the validity of Microcenters as a teacher education strategy, their difficulties, achievements and prospects for the future.

Information was collected through a survey, direct observation and interviews. The sample consisted of 100 teachers from preschool, primary and junior secondary schools from the urban zone in the three Education Districts in the Department of El Huila.

The interview was semi-structured and applied to all teachers in the sample. Both the interviews and the survey addressed three topics: *(a)* teachers' self-image, *(b)* teachers' daily work, and *(c)* training-related factors. Among the latter, the study attempted to identify teachers' understanding and definitions of the Microcenters as a strategy to improve educational quality through teacher training, as well as their failures and achievements, and teachers' suggestions to improve them. Also explored were some conditions of teacher group work, such as levels of participation, the role of the Microcenter coordinator, the reflection process conducted by the group, the relevance of the topics discussed, and the materials used at the Microcenters. In addition, on-site observation greatly widened the scope of the research.

The triad of survey-observation-interviews made it possible to conduct an analysis of the relationship between theory and practice in the development of the Microcenters, given that a specific purpose of the study was to detect inconsistencies and/or coincidences between what was *intended* and what was actually *occurring*.

Teachers' Self-Image

In Colombia the social image of the teaching profession has suffered important deteriorative changes over the last few years. The increasing urbanization process, the crisis in the training of teachers, the deterioration of educational quality, among others, have contributed to lowering the status of teachers. Labour struggles, the contractual character of teaching work, and the rapid and massive expansion of educational services have led to a view of teachers as common workers or wage earners, rather than as cultural workers or citizen builders.

Thus, the survey initially set out to investigate the views of teachers on themselves and on their profession. The range of answers confirmed that the traditional "apostle" image was predominant and persistent (68%), followed by the "wage earner" (27%) and the "cultural worker" (10.3%). Many teachers defined themselves simply as "guides", "friends", "advisors", "trainers", or "instructors." This evinced the lack of reflection by teachers on their current image and status, and on the shifts in societal perceptions of such image and status.

Pre-school teachers provided the following definition: "*The Microcenter is a work team with a common interest: the child. This team gets together to work, plan and organise activities. Each member presents his/her experiences, and alternatives are discussed for working with children and the community. The Microcenter is a supporting and working group of teachers.*

A primary school teacher noted: "*I think that the Microcenter is a gathering of teachers who have a common interest: an interest in engaging in pedagogical reflection. We discuss the problems we have with the children in the classroom and the problems we confront with the community. In this way we exchange our experiences*".

One of the most popular union leaders in the Department of El Huila, and Director of the Center for Educational Studies and Research (CEID), said: "*I see the Microcenter as a collective workshop that facilities the development of teaching in as much as the teacher experience is not only retrieved but is socially processed through the Microcenter*".

Teachers' Understanding of the Microcenters

The survey and the interviews revealed that teachers had a good grasp of the concept of the Microcenter as a place for pedagogical reflection, where they can speak up and open their practice to public observation. However, teachers viewed the Microcenter not only as a venue for training but also as a tool for organising school work. Both dimensions—learning, and horizontal cooperative work among teachers—mark a breakthrough in conventional teacher education and work practices, and an important step forward in the professional autonomy of teachers.

Another important aspect deals with how teachers perceive the differences between what they called "*traditional training*" and "*training through the Microcenters*", with a clearly favourable preference for the latter. The survey revealed the following teacher perceptions:

TEACHER'S PERCEPTIONS	
Traditional in-service training	**In-service training through Microcenters**
Centered on lecturing. Teacher's experience is not acknowledged.	Participatory and lively. Professional experience is valued as the main source for improved and continuous learning.
Courses are too theoretical.	Knowledge acquired at the Microcenter is put into practice.
Work is done in isolation.	Group work is fostered.
Attendance is for the purpose of acquiring credit	Credit is the result of a work of reflection and action.
Deficient evaluation and follow up.	Self-evaluation is fostered. Teachers are encouraged to generate new learning.

Teachers' Group Work At the Pedagogical Workshop

By stimulating an exchange of experiences the Microcenters imply group work and a cooperative relationship among teachers. However, forming groups of teachers and promoting collective reflection, discussion and exchange is not an easy task given the traditional isolation and lack of such opportunities offered to teachers in the past. Successive education reforms and decentralization processes have increasingly individualized teachers.

This is precisely one of the dilemmas faced by the Microcenters. In order to explore gains and difficulties in this domain, teachers were asked to describe how the Microcenters were operating in each case.

However, analyses by teachers who were interviewed and direct observations at some Microcenters revealed a major difficulty in such group work: the role of the coordinator in the working sessions. Once the group decides who is the most charismatic or the most qualified (or better able, for any other reason), there is no rotation. This generates dependency and leads inevitably to routine.

Difficulties and Misconceptions

One of the most common misconceptions among technicians from the MEN and teachers was considering the Microcenters exclusively centered around Curricular Renewal. Moreover, direct observation revealed that the work at the Microcenters was focused on formal tasks, chiefly dividing and integrating units of the curriculum, and producing materials. Microcenters with over a year of operation had not surpassed this stage and had fallen into a set routine. There was a lack of attention to the collective reflection practice and teacher demotivation in several Microcenters.

Another difficulty identified by the study was the deep dependence of teachers on State educational agencies. If those institutions failed to deliver materials or advisors, the Microcenters did not take off by themselves. This situation was clearly an expression of a predominantly top-down school culture, where teachers developed no confidence in their own capacities and had lost their sense of initiative.

Clearly, the success of the Microcenters depends not only on the State but on the teachers themselves, on their willingness and capacity to change traditional attitudes, to understand that their professional learning must arise from their needs and interests, and that an improvement in education quality depends largely upon themselves.

Fostering of School Educational Projects

As stated earlier, a specific objective of the Microcenters is to encourage teachers to develop an Educational Project for their respective schools. This project was expected to result from a research programme which would lead to activities of the Microcenter for at least one year.

The study found that there was little clarity on these Educational Projects both among teachers and the MEN technicians. Many confused the Pedagogical Workshop with the Educational Project.

Traditionally teacher training (both pre- and in-service) has not provided teachers with the necessary knowledge and skills for undertaking research. Critics of the Microcenters had argued that it was absurd to expect teachers to conduct research and to become teacher-researchers. However, research at the Microcenters was conceived not as academic research competing with universities and specialized institutions, but research on teachers' work and daily practice. Teacher research was defined as "*rigorous and systematic production of pedagogical knowledge generated by teachers, and aimed at critically analyzing their own practice towards transforming this knowledge into more efficient and democratic ways of teaching and learning*".

ACCOMPLISHMENTS OF THE MICROCENTER STRATEGY

The study revealed the following accomplishments of the Microcenters:

Increased teacher awareness of the deficiencies of traditional training schemes: An important accomplishment was teachers' awareness of the crisis of traditional teacher training and the possibility of alternative schemes. The Microcenters appeared as an alternative with which teachers were ready to experiment.

Recovering the school as a cultural environment for the community: Some Microcenters that had focused on improvements in the area of Language had defined important cultural recuperation projects. Many meetings were attended by parents who shared their cultural traditions, poems, legends, songs and other cultural expressions.

The fact that training is provided *in situ* and teachers are not removed from their daily environment, facilitated the development of teacher creativity and autonomy. Although there were teachers who expressed resistance to the Microcenter, many pointed out its advantages and potential.

Microcenters and School-Clustering in Colombia

An important factor that needs to be considered, and one which facilitated the organisation of the Microcenters in Colombia, is the process of school-clustering (*nuclearización*) that was institutionalized and began to be implemented countrywide back in 1982. Each nucleus is formed by 8 to 15 schools in both urban and rural areas. Each nucleus has an Advisory Committee integrated by community members, and a Technical-Pedagogical Committee comprising teachers and headmasters. The grouping of 15 to 25 nuclei within a homogeneous geographical area forms an Education District, which is the administrative cell at the zone level.

SOME CONCLUSIONS AND RECOMMENDATIONS OF THE STUDY

Researchers concluded that if the misunderstandings and major obstacles can be overcome, the Microcenters have the potential of becoming a successful strategy at regional and national level, facilitating a change in teachers' roles and morale, and the building of an alternative pedagogy in the classrooms.

The study highlighted several conclusions, based on the analysis of the Microcenters conducted in the Department of El Huila:

- Teacher's image, as perceived by teachers, still reflected the archaic notions of the teacher as an *apostle*.
- A traditional absence of reflection on their daily school work prevented teachers from identifying deficiencies in their teaching practice, and their role in school failure. The excessive routinization and ritualization of the teaching practice prevented teachers from seeing the importance of pedagogical reflection at the Microcenters.
- Teachers in the Department of El Huila had little, partial and superficial information and understanding of the Curricular Renewal. Reflecting this, the work at the Microcenters was eminently focused on formal aspects of such Curricular

Renewal, disregarding the study and analysis of its theoretical framework and the wide social debate held in the country on its nature and orientation.

- Group association and collaboration, essential to the effective functioning of the Microcenters, faced serious difficulties due to the secular isolation of the teacher's role.
- Lack of clarity on the role of the Microcenter had led to confusion between the *Pedagogical Workshop* and the *Educational Project.*
- Some teachers, head teachers and officials displayed a bureaucratic understanding of the Microcenters, viewing them as places where they could fill out forms. Few had understood the integral role of the Microcenter as an environment for pedagogical reflection and knowledge.
- Due to misconceptions, teachers were not able to define clearly the role of the Microcenter coordinator.
- Evaluation was found to be the weakest point of the work at the Microcenters because it was approached in a mechanical and traditional way.
- The achievements of the Microcenters in the Department of El Huila were meaningful but it was not possible to state, at the point, that they were a success.

RECOMMENDATIONS

The following recommendations were proposed, within the framework of the educational reform in progress in the country:

- It is essential to overcome short-sighted views of the Microcenter and to consider it instead as a multifaceted strategy for teacher sharing, pedagogical reflection and discussion on a wide spectrum of issues related to their profession and the improvement of the school system.
- Administrative considerations must be avoided when approaching the Microcenters as a strategy for teachers'

pedagogical reflection and experimentation. The State's educational agencies must provide the Microcenters logistical support but provide them the conceptual and methodological autonomy that is essential for their development.

- Microcenters should intersperse horizontal encounters among teachers with high quality courses linked to their daily situation and needs, so as to enhance to conditions for improving reflection and transforming action.
- If the Microcenters are considered a viable alternative for fostering teacher empowerment, teachers' image should be a topic of specific discussion among teachers at the Pedagogical Workshop. This is a pre-condition for teacher awareness of the problems facing education and of the need to work collectively towards a more professional and autonomous role.
- Rotation in the coordination role at the Microcenters is a must. Technicians from the MEN should make this absolutely clear and orient teachers accordingly, providing them guidelines on the role of the coordinator (such as provoking participation rather than monopolizing expression, encouraging discussion and accepting different points of view rather than trying to reach hasty and superficial agreements, etc.).
- If teachers are expected to research their own pedagogical practice and to elaborate educational projects for the schools, they need to be provided with basic conceptual and methodological tools. This is preceded by the need for addressing the training of trainers who can assist teachers in the elaboration and follow-up of such projects.
- The work at the Microcenters should be supported by the provision of texts and audiovisual materials. Microcenters tend to veer towards routine in the absence of such materials.

- The State educational bodies (such as the Ministry of Education and the Experimental Pilot Centers) must perceive the Microcenters as objects of research and permanent evaluation. Rigorous research is important to enable a better understanding of the processes and mechanisms involved in teacher education and professional improvement, if the Microcenters intend to become a true teacher training alternative.
- There is a need to strengthen the linkages between the Microcenters and universities and higher education institutions, particularly for research and training purposes. Linkages between universities and the teaching practice feeds the academic processes of the university, benefits teachers and their training, and acknowledges the protagonistic role of the community and civil society.
- It is necessary to stimulate inter-institutional efforts in order to pool resources for education reform, and for teacher training reform in particular.
- It must be acknowledged that substantive changes in teacher education strategies are not achieved by top-down rules but through a process that implies the spurring of new educational practices seeking teachers' autonomy and identity, and an overall improvement in the quality of education.
- National teacher training policies must be backed by research and systematic evaluation in order to analyze their achievements and difficulties, and introduce timely and strategic correctives where necessary.

Sources

- César Vera and Francisco Parra, "Microcenters and Teacher Education". in: *Bulletin* N° 22, UNESCO-OREALC, Santiago, 1990.
- Rosa Avila Aponte, "Alternatives en la formación permanente: Microcentros rurales y escuelas demostrativas",

en: *Cómo aprende y cómo enseña el docente. Un debate sorbe el perfeccionamiento*, PIIE/ICE, Santiago, 1992.

- Ministerio de Educación (MEN), *Boletín de los CEP*, Nº 9, Bogota, Marzo 1986.
- María Margarita López Castaño, "La descentralización educativa en Colombia" en: V: Espínola (editora), *La construcción de lo local en los sistemas educativos descentralizados: Los casos de Argentina, Brasil, Chile y Colombia*, CIDE, Santiago, 1994.

—Rosa-Maria Torres UNICEF
Courtesy: UNICEF and UNESCO,
Education For All: Making it Work

4

The Training Strategy of the National Literacy Campaign "Monsignor Leonidas Proaño"

Training is a particularly neglected, often outdated and tedious area within the adult literacy field. Seeking to overcome this traditional weakness, the literacy campaign described here placed central importance on the initial and on-the-job training and support of young literacy teachers and introduced several innovative aspects. A general background is provided, followed by a specific description of the training component.

The Campaign

The "Monsignor Leonidas Proaño" National Literacy Campaign (1988–1990) was undertaken as a joint responsibility of the Ministries of the Social Front (Education, Social Welfare, Health, and Labour), and was coordinated by the Ministry of Education (MEC). Named after a renowned Ecuadorian Bishop and human rights advocate, the campaign aimed at contributing to a broad-based educational discussion in the country in order to change and revitalize the formal school system.

Two separate campaigns were undertaken, one for the Spanish-speaking population and one for the Quechua-speaking population. The latter campaign was designed and coordinated by the National Division of Intercultural Indigenous Bilingual Education–DINEIIB, created in 1988, and had its own calendar, curricula, and training plan. Only the Spanish campaign will be described here.

Stages the Campaign had three stages:

I. Design, planning and organisation

II. Implementation

III. Systematization and final evaluation

Objectives: The campaign never made claims of "eradicating" illiteracy in the country, but of teaching as many people as possible to read and write, and to ensure a level of literacy that would enable them to continue learning on their own if they so desired. Strong emphasis was therefore placed on the pedagogical issues involved in literacy instruction. Learning achievement results revealed that over 80% of the students who completed the campaign were able to comprehensively read and write a personal letter to their literacy educator.

The objectives of the campaign were formulated as follows:

- To teach reading and writing to the largest possible number of illiterate and semi-literate youth and adults in the country;
- To educate secondary school students in Ecuador's social problems and provide them with an opportunity to be socially useful, by involving them as literacy teachers;
- To promote national information and awareness on human rights, including the right to education;
- To influence the regular school system through the active involvement of students, their teachers and parents in the campaign, and through the development and dissemination of new educational approaches and methods, particularly regarding literacy teaching;

- To initiate national discussion on the country's educational problems and encourage a widespread social movement in favor of education reform.

Premises: The campaign was based on the following premises:

- Illiteracy is a structural problem which cannot be resolved by means of one single action. Reaching the literacy goal requires sustained actions linked to an integral national education policy that guarantees access, equality and quality in education.

- The illiteracy issue includes *functional illiteracy*. A literacy action must also deal with the latter.

- Human Rights provide a highly valuable and significant universal content for literacy instruction and for encouraging a democratic, critical and mobilizing education process. Human Rights provide also a common framework to the different topics dealt with in a literacy process, which are otherwise presented in a scattered and isolated manner.

- A massive literacy action can become a privileged tool to incite a broad-based national education movement capable of arousing awareness, critical reflection and national debate around education so as to impact on the formal education system, its agents, conceptions, methodologies and practices.

- Youth are a highly productive, untapped social force. A massive educational action such as a literacy campaign requires the mobilization of non-conventional social and teaching forces, and gives youth an invaluable forum for social participation, expression and learning.

- The role of the educator is the determining factor in the education process. Special attention must thus be given to the education and training of educators themselves through a permanent, systematic and integrated strategy that draws upon diverse modalities and means.

Literacy Educators: 72,753 educators participated in the Campaign, the majority of whom were students in their final years of high school. Student participation as literacy educators was established as a prerequisite for graduation, replacing the conventional thesis. The remainder comprised rural teachers, volunteers, and adult educators from the Adult Education Division of the MEC. Literacy educators were organised in 3,230 *brigades* (teams of 15 to 30 students), both rural and urban. Brigades were coordinated by secondary school or university teachers.

A two-pronged training plan was designed for the literacy educators. Training lasted 8 months and featured both distance modalities (32 booklets that were produced and distributed weekly) and face-to-face modalities (one-week workshops organised around instructional videos especially prepared for the campaign).

In order to facilitate adult enrolment and learning, each secondary school involved in the campaign was instructed to form two types of brigades: some dedicated to literacy instruction, and others to providing support, such as taking care of young children while their parents—especially mothers—attended classes.

Literacy Students: The last (1982) population census estimated that there were 826,485 illiterates over 15 years of age out of an overall population of 10 million inhabitants (an official 13.9% illiteracy rate). A total of 350,000 literacy students, including children, youth and adults, were enrolled in rural and urban areas. As expected, although 12 years was established as the minimum age, many children under that age enrolled and many learned together with their parents. Literacy educators were instructed to organise separate groups for children, youth and adults whenever possible.

The campaign addressed the needs of both the illiterate and the semi-literate (with some school experience, but with weak reading and writing skills). Pedagogical orientations included peer-tutoring, with those with some school experience helping their less advanced classmates. Learning results of the campaign, however, showed no significant differences between those enrolled with some previous school experience and those with none. Thus, the campaign contributed to further underscore the low quality of learning in the regular school system.

Literacy Sites: 25,729 *Círculos de Alfabetización Popular-CAP* (Popular Literacy Circles) were organised throughout the country in rural and urban areas. These CAPs operated in any available building (schools, churches, homes, community houses, etc.) or in the open air.

Literacy Content, Pedagogy and Materials: Human Rights was adopted as the overall framework and content of the campaign. The 12 lessons of the primer *Nuestros Derechos* (Our Rights) were developed around the Universal Declaration of Human Rights—each lesson refers to one or a group of related human rights. The training of literacy educators also focused on Human Rights and encouraged them to compare rights against Ecuador's realities in the fields of health, nutrition, education, gender equality, free expression, and so on. Thus, the campaign constituted a learning experience and a practical exercise in human rights not only for illiterates but for the literacy educators and Ecuadorian society as a whole.

Approaches and methodologies proposed for literacy teaching incorporated updated trends in literacy instruction and acquisition, and benefitted from recent research in this field. The preparation of literacy materials was based on an analysis of a large sample of literacy materials previously produced and used in Ecuador and Latin America.

Literacy Implementation: The literacy process lasted 4 months (May-September 1989). The Literacy Follow-Up Plan had two components: administrative and pedagogical. The following activities were included within the Pedagogical Follow-Up:

(a) meetings of literacy educators at the parish, zone and provincial level, culminating with a National Congress held in Quito at the end of the campaign (September 1989);

(b) meetings of brigade coordinators (secondary school teachers) at the provincial and national level; and

(c) a national radio programme with pedagogical orientations which was broadcast nationally on weekends during the 4-month literacy periods.

The Campaign and Education Reform: Capitalizing on the social dynamics brought about by a massive and intensive national undertaking such as this, the national literacy campaign was perceived as an education movement aimed at provoking critical reflection and extensive debate around the educational issue, beyond the confines of adult literacy and adult education. Thus:

- the campaign was designed and implemented by the Ministry of Education (MEC), and involved Universities and NGOs related to the education issue throughout the country;
- secondary school students were the main literacy teaching force;
- secondary school teachers were the coordinators of the student brigades;
- all materials prepared for the campaign—including the training materials—were distributed to the entire MEC staff, primary schools, primary school teachers, and teacher associations;
- specific training plans were designed for each of the groups involved in the campaign: secondary school students, secondary school teachers, and MEC staff at the local, intermediate and central level; and
- the campaign culminated with a National Congress of the Literacy Educators, where these secondary school students were asked to analyze the national education system and make proposals for change.

The Evaluation of the Campaign: Two complementary evaluations were conducted: *(a)* an *internal evaluation*, from the perspective of the literacy *educators* (a final questionnaire was distributed to all literacy educators prior to the conclusion of the campaign); and *(b)* an *external evaluation*, from the perspective of the literacy *students,* centered around learning achievement (a literacy test was applied to 3,011 literacy students) and including an evaluation of impact at the community level (perceptions by local authorities such as priests and other community members).

The results of both evaluations were published separately and jointly, and were widely disseminated within and outside the country. Some significant results of the perceptions of the literacy educators:

- 95.3% of the literacy educators said that the Universal Declaration of Human Rights should be adopted as the content for future literacy/education actions;
- 98.5% said that they had gained the confidence and affection of their students; 72.5% said they had received support from community leaders; and 66.6% said they had engaged in community work.
- 98.6% assessed their participation in the campaign as interesting or very interesting; 64.4% said that what they learned would be very useful to their own personal development; 90.7% said that the experience enabled them to learn a great deal about their own capabilities.
- 95.1% recommended that secondary school students be regularly involved in adult literacy programmes and campaigns.

Costs: The cost of the (Spanish and Quechua) campaign was assumed by the Ecuadorian government and amounted a total of 3.107,891 *sucres* (500 sucres per US dollar at that time). International collaboration came from AECI (Spain Cooperation Agency), ICT, UNDP, UNESCO, and UNICEF.

Some Notable Tensions and Obstacles

- The argument that priority should be given to the education of children over adult education.
- The defense of a professional teaching certificate as pre-requisite for teaching and, as a corollary, the lack of confidence on young secondary school students as being apt for this task.
- The lack of updated, consistent and reliable statistical data on the situation of education in general, and on adult literacy in particular.

- The eminently quantitative concerns of politicians, educational authorities and the media: the main concern (and criterion to evaluate the campaign) and *how many* and *how much* (enrolment, literacy rates, costs, etc.) with little attention to process, quality and effective learning.
- The resistance to innovation not only within the education sector but in families and society at large.
- Mutual resistance between State, NGOs, and community organisations, which hindered progress and coordination.

Conclusion: The 1998-1990 Ecuadorian literacy campaign showed that this type of action—massive, with broad-based social participation and focused on the mobilization of youth—is possible and proves socially productive in conditions other than revolutionary processes, traditionally viewed as prototypes for such endeavours.

In 1989, the literacy educators of the campaign received the Latin American Human Rights Award granted by the Latin American Association for Human Rights (ALDHU). In 1990, the campaign was selected by UNESCO as one of five adult literacy experiences to be presented at a special panel during the "World Conference on Education for All" in Jomtien, Thailand.

The campaign was continued through a regular Adult Basic Education (ABE) programme equivalent to primary education.

THE TRAINING PLAN OF THE LITERACY EDUCATORS

Weaknesses of Teachers Training within the Adult Literacy Field

The concept and design of the campaign were based on a critical analysis of literacy experiences conducted in Ecuador and other developing countries. The campaign aimed at overcoming weaknesses habitually found in such experiences, particularly in two areas: training and evaluation.

Training was viewed as key to the campaign success, indispensable not only for the literacy educators but for the entire MEC structure and campaign staff at the national, provincial and local level. Specifically, the training strategy aimed at reversing some of the problems and narrow approaches that have characterized the conventional training model within the adult literacy field (*see box*).

Some Training Premises of the Campaign

- It is not enough to know something in order to be able to teach it to others. *Learning to teach* is essential.
- Adult education, and adult literacy in particular, is a specific area within the education field, and necessitates specific knowledge and competencies.
- It is not enough to be a teacher in order to be able to teach adults to read and write. Certified teachers, trained to teach children, need to learn how to teach adults.
- The adult education field is in continuous change. Much relevant knowledge has been produced over the last three decades, outdated knowledge has been rectified, new theoretical proposals have emerged, empirical experience has been gained. The adults of today are different from those of the mid-1990s. The social, political, economical and specially educational realities of the world, and of each country in particular, have undergone major changes. All these factors make it essential to upgrade and rejuvenate the knowledge accumulated within the field.

Preparing good literacy teachers require:

- understanding training as a process, going beyond the single, initial, isolated event;
- overcoming the bent for "methods" and "techniques" that predominate in the field, aiming at an integral approach—pedagogical and social, theoretical and practical—thus avoiding the repetition of well-known cliches in the field of literacy;

- overcoming the tendency to replicate "models", seeking and identifying the specific conditions of each programme, its organisation, means, contents and methodologies;
- stimulating self-study and continuous education and training, linked to the needs that emerge from practice; and
- making pedagogical practice a source and tool for continuous learning.

The Conventional Training Model of Adult Literacy Actions

- *Neglect of the training component* within an overall neglect of the human resources involved at different levels. More emphasis is placed on material inputs and educational technology than on capacity building and teaching-learning conditions. It is assumed that teaching reading and writing (to both adults and children) is a fairly simple task, not requiring specific knowledge or skills.
- *Short and asystematic training efforts*, usually reduced to a lone event—a short workshop or seminar—in the absence of a strategic and systemic training plan. Training is typically offered *before* the literacy programme begins, with little or no attention to continuous on-the-job support and upgrading.
- *An instrumental and narrow approach to training*. Training is centered around a particular literacy "method" or a specific primer or manual, with little attention paid to the understanding of literacy pedagogy, the students, and the context. Moreover, so-called literacy "methods" are often not methods at all, and replicate conventional child literacy instruction in schools. Both learners' and teachers' materials tend to be rigid and prescriptive, following a given sequence of steps. The teacher's guide or manual is meant to compensate for the weaknesses of the teachers' profile and the training programme.
- *Neglect of pedagogical aspects in favour of administrative ones*. Training habitually devotes more importance and time to administrative rather than pedagogical issues related to the literacy programme.

- *Neglect of pedagogical aspects in favour of broader "sociological" ones.* In progressive programmes, particularly those inspired by Paulo Freire's ideas—awareness-building, "dialogue" on aspects of learners' reality, etc.—it is common to find that the social, ideological, cultural and ideological dimensions of illiteracy and literacy overshadow the specific pedagogic dimension of teaching and learning to read and write.
- *Little linkage with practice.* Despite common rhetoric to the contrary, training stems from a *priori* definitions on training and on training learning needs regarding both content and pedagogy.
- *Homogeneous and model-oriented training.* The training curriculum and the administration and organisation of training programmes within the adult literacy field are very similar around the world. They tend to replicate conventional patterns and models, without an analysis of the specific conditions, objectives and agents involved in the training programme.
- *Lack of systematization and evaluation of the training programme*, which typically remains undocumented and unanalyzed in its results and impact on trainees and on learners. In evaluated, results are not incorporated into improving further training or sharing lessons learned with others.
- *Lack of innovation* Training is adult literacy programmes remains essentially tied to the ancient wisdom generated within the adult literacy field and lacks contact with the new knowledge produced both within and outside the field.
- *Training centered around written materials and print*, including the material for the learner (a primer, a reading book) and the manual or guide for the teacher. There is little exploration of other training strategies including audio and visual materials.
- *Residential training provides the prototype*, with little exploration and development of distance learning possibilities.

THE TRAINING PLAN OF THE CAMPAIGN

The training plan, under the responsibility of the Pedagogical Direction of the campaign, lasted 8 months and combined distance and face-to-face modalities. Training was initiated 5 months prior to the commencement of the literacy process, and continued throughout the literacy process, until the closure of the campaign.

Characteristics of the Training Plan

The training plan was defined as:

- *National:* For all. Addressed not only to the literacy educators but to the entire personnel of the campaign, from the national to the local level;
- *Permanent:* Conducted both before and during the literacy process, in order to enable educators to continuously upgrade their knowledge and competencies, and to contrast theory with practice;
- *Integral:* Including both the pedagogical and the social aspects of literacy teaching;
- *Collective:* Promoting dialogue and exchange, the formation of study groups, reflection and discussion, both in the residential and in the distance modalities;
- *Critical:* Rejecting passiveness and rote learning on the part of both teachers and learners. Aimed at developing, in both, the capacity to reason, to critically analyze and discuss that which is taught;
- *Multiplying:* From a few to many, through to a pyramid strategy in which each one shares with others what she or he has learned;
- *Differentiated:* Each group according to its own needs, acknowledging the heterogeneity of educational agents and of tasks involved at various levels and in different situations;
- *Flexible:* Each group according to its possibilities, allowing great flexibility in terms of content, modalities, approaches and calendars within the national training framework.

A. THE DISTANCE MODALITY

The *distance* modality was implemented through *(a)* a collection of weekly *Working Documents* (32 booklets), and *(b)* a radio programme with pedagogical orientations.

The Working Documents

32 Working Documents were produced and distributed weekly throughout the country for 8 months, with a circulation of 200,000. Specially designed plastic bags were distributed so that the booklets could be easily collected and carried along.

The distribution of such booklets started 5 months prior to the literacy period. They played an important role in information and in addressing key questions about the campaign among future literacy educators. They provided them with basic knowledge and tools to prepare themselves for the challenge ahead: contact with an unknown community, the reality of poverty and illiteracy, the psychology of an adult learner, the pedagogy of literacy. As evaluated by literacy educators, these booklets helped them gain confidence in themselves and reduced the anxieties nurtured by their families and society at large who believed that young students, non-certified teachers, would not be able to teach.

The Working Documents were conceived as materials for group work. The last page of each booklet contained a specific *Guide for Group Work* which included a number of questions aimed at provoking group reflection and analysis. Secondary schools were asked to devote two hours per week to have students (future literacy educators) study and work on the week's document together with their classmates and the teacher appointed as brigade coordinator.

Acknowledging the poor reading habits of young students in the country, and of the literate population in general, the Working Documents were short (between 16 and 24 pages) and special attention was given to the language used and the graphic design (illustrated with photographs, drawings and cartoons). In a way, such materials were meant as a literacy plan for the literacy teachers themselves. An intermediate evaluation of the use of these materials, conducted halfway into the campaign, confirmed the low literacy levels and poor reading habits of the future school graduates.

The Literacy Educators' Library (32 Working Documents)

Document	Series	Title
1.	Information	General Guidelines on the Campaign
2.	Information	Learning to Teach: The Training of the Literacy Educators of the Campaign
3.	Information	Can Young Students Teach Reading and Writing?
4.	History of Literacy	The UNP-LAE Literacy Campaign (1944–1961)
5.	Social	Universal Declaration of Human Rights
6.	Pedagogical	The Educational Conception of the Campaign
7.	Monsignor Proaño	Monsignor Proaño: His Message through Anecdotes
8.	History of Literacy	The State Assumes Responsibility for Literacy: The 1963–1972 Literacy Programme
9.	Pedagogical	The Teaching and Learning Materials of the Campaign
10.	Monsignor Proaño	Monsignor Proaño and Literacy: The Popular Radiofonic Schools (ERPE)
11–12	Pedagogical	The Learning and Teaching of the Written Language

13	History of Literacy	The Functional Literacy Pilot Project (1967–1972)
14.	Pedagogical	The Qualities of the Educator (Paulo Freire)
15.	Social	What is the Situation of Housing in Ecuador?
16–17	Pedagogical	The Literacy Educator as a Community Educator.
18	Social	What is the Situation of Indigenous Nationalities in Ecuador?
19.	Pedagogical	What One is NOT Supposed to Do in the Literacy Process
20	Monsignor Proaño	Being Young (Monsignor Leonidas Proaño)
21	Social	What Happens With the Situation of the Environment in Ecuador?
22–23	Information	National Literacy Follow-Up Plan (May-September 1989)
24	Social	What is the Situation of Health in Ecuador?
25	Social	What is the Situation of Children in Ecuador?
26.	Social	What is the Situation of Women in Ecuador?
27	Social	What is the Situation of Education in Ecuador?
28–29	Pedagogical	In Levity and Seriousness: Reviewing our Education
30–31	History of Literacy	The National Literacy Programme "Jaime Roldós Aguilera" (1980–1984)
32	Social	What is the Situation of the Land in Ecuador?

These booklets included five different thematic series, each identified with a specific colour (*see detail in box*):

1. *Information About the Campaign* (5 booklets): This series provided general guidelines on the campaign, and on its development.

2. *The Thinking of Monsignor Leonidas Proaño* (4 booklets): This series dwelt on the biography, ideas and work of the bishop after whom the campaign was named.

3. *The History of Literacy in Ecuador* (4 booklets): A systematic account was provided on the various literacy actions undertaken in the country since 1944, when the first literacy campaign was held. The series was based on interviews.

4. *The Pedagogical Dimension of Literacy* (10 booklets): This series offered pedagogical knowledge related to the field of literacy in general, and of adult literacy in particular. One booklet featured the problems of Ecuador's education system and was entirely based on cartoons.

5. *The Social Dimensions of Literacy* (9 booklets): This series began with the Universal Declaration of Human Rights, followed by an analysis of rights implementation in the country in various areas: education, health, housing, equal rights between men and women, free expression, etc.

A weekly radio programme A radio programme with pedagogical orientations was broadcast for the literacy educators on Saturdays, and repeated on Sundays, throughout the literacy process.

B. THE FACE-TO FACE MODALITY

The residential modality was implemented through two mechanisms: *(a)* a one-week workshop before the start of the campaign, and *(b)* weekly meetings of literacy educators throughout the literacy period.

THE FACE-TO-FACE TRAINING PLAN

Pedagogical Direction of the Campaign

Workshop 1 (Quito, January) Provincial directors and national supervisors of the regular school system		

Workshop 2 (Provinces, January) Provincial supervisors of the regular school system		

Workshop 3	**Workshop 4**	**Workshop 5**
(Quito, Feb-March) Provincial directors and provincial pedagogical teams	(Quito, March) Selected secondary and normal school teachers	(Provinces, March-April) District directors and district pedagogical teams

Workshop 6	**Workshop 7**
(Provinces, April) Secondary school teachers at the province level	(Quito, April) Promoters of workers' and community organisations

Workshops for Literacy Educators
(throughout the country, April-May)

In each provincial or district of the campaign	In each secondary or normal school	In each organization
Regular staff of the Adult Education Department of MEC Volunteers	Students	Promoters of workers' and community organizations

The Training Workshops

Face-to-face training focused on the pedagogical issues of literacy teaching. It followed a cascade approach, with a multiplier mechanism at national, provincial and local levels, and concluded with the workshops for the literacy educators.

Videos for the Training Workshops: In order to avoid typical problems associated with multiplier or "cascade" approaches, four videos were prepared by the Pedagogical Division of the campaign for use in these workshops. The videos were accompanied by a brief *Video Orientation Guide*. As with the *Working Documents*, the videos proposed a group use methodology, promoting group reflection and analysis. Each campaign office at provincial level was provided a betamax unit.

Four Lines of Training: Four different lines of training were organised, acknowledging the specific nature of four groups with different roles within the campaign:

- *(a)* MEC staff linked to the National Division of Regular and Special Education, including National Supervisors (who would be integrated in information and organisational/ administrative follow-up tasks) and Provincial Education Directors (who would be part of the Provincial Executive Committees of the Campaign);
- *(b)* MEC staff linked to the Division of Adult Education—DINEPP, who would be the Provincial and District Pedagogical Directors of the campaign;
- *(c)* secondary school teachers, who would integrate the School Literacy Committees and would be Coordinators of the Student Literacy Brigades; and
- *(d)* promoters and leaders of community organisations, who would conduct the literacy campaign within their own organisations.

A specific agenda was drawn-up for each line and for each level of training.

Workshops for Literacy Educators: The entire training plan culminated in the workshops for literacy educators. These were facilitated by pedagogical teams at the provincial and zone levels, aided by the videos. Workshops were held at various places: campaign offices, secondary schools, communal houses, etc.

Two alternative calendar options were offered: modality A, with one full week of training; and modality B, consisting of five consecutive Saturdays. Workshop calendars also differed for the four regions in the country: Coast (between end of March and first week of April); Highlands; the Amazon Region; and Galápagos (between April and May).

Weekly Meetings

Throughout the literacy teaching-learning process, and as part of the follow up of the campaign, meetings between student educators were promoted at the parish, zone and provincial levels. These concluded with the National Congress of Literacy Educators, held in Quito after the conclusion of the campaign. Nearly 1,000 student-teachers from the entire country attended as delegates of their respective brigades.

Weekly meetings were also promoted among teachers who coordinated the brigades, culminating with meetings at the provincial and national levels.

Evaluation of the Training Plan of the Campaign

A few weeks before the conclusion of the literacy process, a National Evaluation Questionnaire was distributed to all literacy educators, to be completed before they ended their assignment. The survey sought information on all aspects of the campaign, on the personal experience of the literacy educators and on their learners. A specific section was devoted to the training plan. The following is a summary of the conclusions of this evaluation on the implementation of the training plan.

Training Workshops

- 93.3% of the literacy educators participated in the workshops organised by the campaign;

- 21.3% considered the workshop excellent, 45.9% very good, 27.9% good, 4.0% fair, and 0.9% poor;

- 40.9% considered the workshop to be very useful, 56.4% useful and 2.7% useless.

Videos

- 69.7% utilized the videos in their workshop.

Working Documents

- ***Received:*** 81.7% received all 32 Working Documents.
- ***Read:*** 22% read all of them; 25.9% read between 20 and 29; 32.5% between 10 and 19; 15.5% between 1 and 9; and 4.2% none (students from religious schools had a slightly higher average and private schools the lowest).
- ***Impact on Literacy Learning Achievement:*** There was a direct relationship between the number of documents read by the literacy educators and the literacy levels of their students. Literacy educators who read no documents placed 43.3% of their students in the "fair" achievement level. Those who read 30 documents or more placed 77.9% of their students in that level.
- ***General Opinion:*** 17.8% considered the Working Documents excellent, 50.4% very good, 27.9% good, 3.6% fair, and 0.3% poor. 30.8% considered they were very useful, 65.5% useful, and 3.6% useless to their teaching task. Educators who found them the most useful came from public schools, and were located in the Amazon region, the most isolated region in the country.

The Pedagogical Series was considered most useful. The least popular series among literacy teachers was the Series on History of Literacy in Ecuador.

The series on Monseñor Leonidas Proaño was considered the most interesting and the series on History of Literacy elicited the least interested.

Sources

- Rosa-María Torres, *El Nombre de Ramona Cuji: Reportajes de la Campaña Nacional de Alfabetización "Monseñor*

Leonidas Proaño" (Junio-Septiembre 1989), ALDHU-Editorial El Conejo, Quito, 1990.

—*Alfabetización y Derechos Humanos: La Campaña "Monseñor Leonidas Proaño" del Ecuador*, Quito, 1993.

- Campaña Nacional "Monseñor Leonidas Proaño", Documento de Trabajo N° 1, *Lineamientos generales de la campaña*, Quito, Noviembre 1988.
- —Documento de Trabajo N° 2, *Aprender para enseñar: La formación de los educadores de la campaña*, Quito, Diciembre 1988.
- Campaña Nacional de Alfabetización "Monseñor Leonidas Proaño" —UNICEF, *Informe de Evaluación Final de la Campaña*, Quito, 1990.

—Rosa-Maria Torres/UNICEF
Courtesy: UNICEF and UNESCO,
Education For All: Making It Work

5

The National In-Service Teacher Education Programme and the Community School Day Programme

In 1979, the New Jewel Movement (NJM)—led by Maurice Bishop—took power in Grenada, a small island in the English-speaking Caribbean (total population 110,000 inhabitants), following nearly three decades of dictatorship under the rule of Eric Gairy. Although Grenada had gained its independence in 1974, the Gairy regime had reinforced colonial tendencies.

This was reflected in a number of ways, including the prevalence of a highly elitist school system: few had access (there were 65 primary schools, one secondary school and one university on the island); costs were high; and entrance to the single secondary school and single university was severely restricted. Overall, the educational scene was characterized by high illiteracy and semi-literacy rates among adults; lack of educational opportunities for children; untrained and underpaid teachers; overpopulated primary schools; and expensive secondary and university education. Both the curriculum and the administration of the school system reflected the British structure, with little regard to the social and cultural history and realities of Grenada.

The new government declared 1980 the "Year of Education and Production". As in other revolutionary processes, education would be a cornerstone of the NJM rule. The government committed itself to democratizing education not only by providing access to all, but also by challenging traditional authoritarian relationships in the classroom, and by promoting participatory mechanisms for consultation among teachers, students and the society at large.

Among the government's first programmes were a national literacy campaign, revision of the primary school curriculum, repair of school facilities, construction of the second secondary school in the country, intensive teacher training, reduction of school fees, provision of scholarships for higher education and vocational training programmes.

Three years later, during the "Year of Political and Academic Education" (1983), a review of the economic, political and social issues led to the conclusion that education was the single most important component for the advancement of Grenada. By then, secondary education was free, a national basic adult education programme was underway, the first promotion of newly-trained teachers was imminent, a variety of work-study programmes were under operation, and more than 200 Grenadians were studying overseas for professional careers.

Building Teacher Consensus: The National Teachers' Seminar

One of the first steps taken by the NJM government was the National Teachers' Seminar "*A New Kind of Teacher for a New Society*". The seminar, held in January 1980 and convened by the Ministry of Education, was attended by approximately 1,000 teachers. Teachers at all levels of the system were encouraged to analyze the current state of education and to make suggestions for change. This National Seminar was a critical factor in furthering teacher involvement and support in reforming education in the country.

Teachers' suggestions were published in a booklet entitled "*Teachers Speak*", which would be an important tool in the definition of curricular and pedagogic reform. Although not all of the recommendations were feasible, or applicable at a national level, many ideas helped shape Grenada's education policies and programmes. Some of those proposals helped define two important and inter-related programmes that will be described herein: the National In-Service Teacher Education Programme (NISTEP) and the Community School Day Programme (CSDP). The programmes were based on the following recommendations by teachers:

- establishing a teacher in-service programme;
- organising workshops on the teaching of agriculture, crafts and other vocations at the school level;
- holding local follow-up seminars for teachers;
- preparing new curriculum guides and ensuring circulation to all schools; and
- involving the community in the process of developing the curriculum.

The National In-Service Teacher Education Programme (NISTEP)

Although Grenada's single Teachers' College had been operating for nearly 18 years, by 1979, 68 per cent of primary school teachers were untrained, and more than 70 per cent of secondary school teachers were unqualified. Because of low salaries and lack of incentives, the majority of the 25 teachers who graduated annually from the Teachers' College stopped working as such within a short time. Most considered teaching as a means of subsistence, a temporary job while getting something better or an avenue out of the country. Many viewed the school as a place for intellectual work, and rejected any possibility of including agriculture or crafts within the school curriculum.

The *National In-Service Teacher Education Programme* (NISTEP) was initiated in October 1980 to train primary school teachers, who numbered about 550 at the time. The planning stage was extensive and involved many players in the educational arena. Meetings were held in every parish for teachers and headmasters to discuss the programme proposals. Workshops were held with representatives of the Grenada Teachers' Union. Teachers' College and the University of the West Indies' (UWI) School of Education, to discuss the feasibility of the programme and ways in which to structure it for accreditation by the university. Some UWI officials were skeptical of the programme's viability. The teachers' main concern was that the programme would not be accredited. Finally, UWI agreed to pilot the programme, with the understanding that it would be oriented towards preparing teachers to obtain certification from the university.

NISTEP's goals were to:

- improve pedagogical practices in the classroom;
- increase student achievement outcomes;
- standardize textbooks and develop a national curriculum;
- develop and organise training materials for teacher education;
- upgrade the status of the teaching profession.

NISTEP was managed by a staff of 18 full-time and seven part-time tutors, with expertise or specific subjects. Primary school teachers attended NISTEP one day per week, and during the rest of the week they put into practice in their classrooms what they had learned, under the supervision of teacher-partners, who were qualified teachers.

During the first two years, language arts, mathematics and education were included in the NISTEP curriculum. Social studies, science, agriculture and health education were added in 1983. NISTEP workshops familiarized participants with the new educational policies and gave them an opportunity to build on what they had already developed. *Teachers Speak* was required reading for both trainers and trainees.

Teacher-partners guided and assisted the trainees. They attended at least two lessons presented by the trainees and assessed their performance against standards set by UWI. This on-site assessment facilitated reflection, analysis and improvement of pedagogical practice.

Part of NISTEP's mandate was to evolve as the focal point for developing the new national curriculum. NISTEP subject panel tutors were responsible for working with teachers to develop the new curriculum. This link between professional development and curricular reform provided NISTEP a unique strength and a powerful approach to teacher education.

The Community School Day Programme (CSDP)

CSDP emerged as a complementary programme to NISTEP. During the day that teachers were attending their training, community members were invited to "own" the schools, act as "substitute teachers", and lead cultural and educational activities at the schools and/or at their places or work.

The impetus for CSDP came from some of the teachers' recommendations published in *Teachers Speak:*

- "The school should provide training in handicrafts, woodworking and other vocations".
- "There should be field trips".
- "Children should be exposed to the working environments of fishermen, road construction crews and others".
- "Students should learn how to use plant materials for making toys, ornaments and other useful objects".
- "Children should be taught food and beverage preparation".
- *"Government officials should come to the schools, so that the students can learn more about government"*.

Recommendations such as these reinforced the government's belief that education should be the responsibility of the government as well as of the people. Slogans such as "*If you know, teach; if you don't, learn*" and "*Each one, teach one*" were spread throughout Grenada to heighten collective consciousness on the importance of education and the collective effort required to reform it. This same spirit animated housewives, farm workers, artisans, fishermen, artists, and other community members to share their skills with school students, and made CSDP feasible.

The activities and knowledge shared on CSDP days covered a wide range of subject areas and activities. Both girls and boys were involved in all activities, so as to avoid gender differentiation in terms of conventional male and female roles. Some activities carried out during that one day a week, when the teacher was absent, included:

- cleaning of the school and community;
- field trips to historic or archaeological sites, or to new development projects;
- work assignments with and/or visits to local industries, professional organisations and government offices;
- story-telling or story-reading, dances, songs, theater, puppets, painting, and other forms of culture;
- learning trades, such as masonry, auto mechanics, fishing, basket weaving, and cooking; and
- lectures by community persons in the public sector, business, and civic organisations.

CSDP was critical in *(a)* introducing students to the world of work; *(b)* preparing them to be participants in the process of national development; *(c)* linking school and community in an effective manner, with "community *participation*" acquiring a new and more relevant meaning; *(d)* involving the community and the students in joint development projects; and *(e)* through all these means, providing invaluable inputs and insights to the curriculum development process. The introduction of peer teaching where there were insufficient volunteers from the community was also an important, unexpected development in many schools.

The programme operated through parish coordinators who assisted schools with planning, logistics, organisation and material support, as well as in identifying resource persons. A steering group comprised representatives from various governmental ministries (education, health, development, etc.) served a coordinating function and provided institutional support to the programme.

Locally, CSDP broadened the traditional Parent-Teacher Associations into Community School Councils. The Councils coordinated the school and community inputs, and served to organise those who volunteered their time and knowledge to the school.

Though participation in CSDP, the students' production improved, and crafts, toys and other items were sold to the Grenadian handicraft enterprise (GRENCRAFT), which was created in 1981. Articles of straw, wood, fabric, toys, etc. were exhibited and sold, the proceeds of which benefitted the programme. Several national and two international exhibits were organised with CSDP products. An agricultural school gardens project in 12 primary schools was also created with Oxfam-Canada funding.

CSDP was decentralized in nature, and depended heavily on the quality of cooperation between school and community. Many variables thus affected the performance of this programme: the attitude of school staff and students; the organisational ability of the community programme coordinators; and the commitment of the school headmaster, who remained at the school on CSDP day. The better the headmaster's relationship with the school staff and the community, the more successful the programme became. Dynamic headmasters were creative and dedicated, visiting the volunteers at their homes, holding frequent meetings with the Community School Council, structuring activities well and employing democratic administrative measures.

Through participation in CSDP, student enthusiasm in vocational trades grew, and with it teacher interest in learning more about agriculture, crafts and manual work in general. Although CSDP was originally envisioned as a means of occupying students while their teachers received training, CSDP became a highly inspiring example of productive integration between work and study, and between the school and the community.

Accomplishments and Limitations

The New Jewel Movement (NJM) government aimed at tying education with daily reality and orienting it towards transforming such reality, based on the unity of intellectual and manual labour, theory and practice, school and community. NISTEP and CSDP contributed to these principles, although they did not achieve all the intended goals.

NISTEP

NISTEP trainees improved their knowledge and skills in key areas and helped to shape the new national curriculum. For the first time in Grenada, teachers' opinions and experiences were valued, and teachers were viewed as key to national development.

NISTEP provided educational and professional opportunities for untrained teachers on a national scale—the first programme of its kind in the English-speaking Caribbean. However, an evaluation of the teacher trainees in 1983 raised several areas of concern: some called for the reinstatement of the Teacher's College model; others suggested that the workload of the trainees be reduced; the largest number of suggestions related to improving logistical support to the programme, such as through the provision of transportation, ability-grouping for teachers, and better relationships with and more access to teacher-trainers and tutors.

By 1983, 350 primary teachers were attending NISTEP and had received pay increments and an upgrading of their status. From the inception of the programme, 184 trainees (34.5 per cent) had dropped out of the programme for various reasons. However, for some, the attention was a positive development since it identified early on (rather than at a later stage) those individuals who were not ready to make a commitment to change or who were not prepared to be teachers.

NISTEP was cost-effective. The three-year Teachers' College Programme (1977–1979) amounted to $ 5,659 per student per year whereas NISTEP costs (1981–1983) came to $ 1,848. Additionally, NISTEP trainees had 117 weeks of practice teaching with 39 opportunities for evaluation by a visiting tutor and 117 by a teacher-partner over the three-year training period. In comparison, those in the Teachers' College had 18 weeks of student teaching and only 18 evaluations. Teachers' College trainees received 93 hours of annual training in language arts, mathematics and education. NISTEP teachers had 120 hours in mathematics and language, and 148 in education per year.

NISTEP suffered logistical problems. Staff had heavy schedules and numerous tasks: training teachers, developing the training materials, supervising the trainees in class, and defining new roles for teachers and ideas for changing the conventional curriculum standards. Work overload and time constraints resulted in overlooking some quality aspects.

CSDP

CSDP had also been conceived as being closely associated with the curriculum development process, but this goal was not fully achieved mainly due to insufficient human and financial resources for conducting the necessary research and follow up.

In schools where the programme was well-organised, CSDP yielded excellent results. In general, CSDP was better received and given greater support in rural areas than in urban ones. Rural families and communities were more willing to give of their time, and exhibited a stronger sense of volunteerism. CSDP worked more efficiently when the school headmaster was dynamic and had a good relationship with community members. The success of the programme thus varied from area to area.

In general, CSDP lacked sufficient resources to achieve all its goals. Much of the administration was the responsibility of the Community School Councils, whose members had little or no experience in programme development, classroom management and supervision. Much of the work involved in mobilization of volunteers therefore became the responsibility of school headmasters and Parish Coordinators. The government-level steering group, although committed to the process, could not guarantee the support of the individual ministries to the extent needed to ensure an effective programme. Insufficient training, coordination and financial support were the strongest limitations of the programme.

Conclusions

During the NJM government (1979–1983) educational programmes for improving teacher education had an overall positive impact throughout Grenada. When US troops entered Grenada on October 25, 1983, structures and educational programmes developed by the NJM government were discontinued and expatriate professionals working on these programmes, mainly from other countries in the English-speaking Caribbean, had to leave the country. American volunteers relieved teachers of their duties, and brought in a new curriculum. Adjustments recommended for NISTEP and CSDP were thus not made, nor can their long-term effectiveness be evaluated.

TEACHERS SPEAK

— *"Invite outstanding farmers to come in to the school and talk, with their farming clothes on"*

— *"Training in woodwork, arts and craft to be provided in school. Perhaps some skilled vendors employed to teach"*

— *"Organise field trips to see road construction"*

— *"Expose children to seaport activity, field trips"*

— *"Children should be taught to use indigenous plant material, e.g. seeds, bamboo, for making toys and ornaments"*

— *"Give the children a day for selling what they produce and the money to go towards buying seeds, school supplies, for school repairs, or channel produce into own agro-industry project"*

— *"In the handicraft department of a school children should be taught house-building"*

— *"The woodwork instructor should take a team of boys and go out on weekends or even during their woodwork period doing some repairs to some homes in their village"*

— *"A work-study programme could find scope for the application of skills such as carpentry, woodwork, masonry, joinery, painting. The teaching of these skills in schools will give citizens a certain self-sufficiency in home maintenance"*

- *"Information on roads could be incorporated into several areas of the curriculum: Social Studies, Mathematics (i.e. costs, measurement, etc.)"*
- *"Children can help in road repairs, especially on roads leading to their school. Schools should get into community work. Children can for example collect and sell stones for road repair"*
- *"Educate children fully about the new international airport: cost, funding, advantages, disadvantages"*
- *"Involve children in the building of the airport via schools' saving unions, sale of produce from school gardens, sale of school handicraft—money contributed to airport bonds"*
- *"In the Infant Department: simple experiments, i.e. looking at seeds germinate in a bottle, or giving infants the responsibility of a small kitchen garden"*
- *"Teach children ways of preparing their own produce and let them eat it"*
- *"Involve all children in the preparation of food—boys and girls"*
- *"Children can themselves prepare fruit juices for school breaks"*
- *"Different sections of the working people should be used to teach each other, e.g. farmer lecturing to teacher"*
- *"Schools should be allowed either to print and circulate a school newspaper, or be allowed to contribute articles for a national unbiased newspaper"*
- *"Education should prepare people for decision-making and should produce a situation where all of us can help shape the policy of our country. For this we need to be informed"*
- *"Children should be exposed to democracy in schools. Encourage democratic discussions"*
- *"Self-expression should be encouraged in children. At the same time educate parents who tend to hush their children up"*

- *"Children and the community should be aware of all types of social systems, so that they can draw their own conclusions"*
- *"Develop a school policy. Show pupils how the policy of the school can be related to the communities and then the world"*
- *"Give children information on, and conduct with, children of other Third World countries"*
- *"Children should be permitted and encouraged to set their own standards. Children should make class rules"*
- *"More space on time-table for agriculture, not just a Friday afternoon subject"*
- *"Tourism to be included under Social Studies"*
- *"Develop positive attitudes towards tourists; see the tourist as a person just like oneself, not a 'whiteman', a millionaire, or a money machine"*
- *"Tourists should be invited to visit schools, whenever practicable"*
- *"Teach children a little about the tourist's country, given them an idea of their language and geography"*
- *"Children in the fishing areas should be engaged in actual fishing and marketing fish"*
- *"Teach children boat-building theory"*
- *"Make students aware of the vast amounts spent on imported meats and the dire need for development of our own livestock industry in order to boost the economy"*
- *"Involve children in livestock rearing: infants could rear chickens; juniors sheep, goats; seniors, cows"*
- *"We need to be informed about Grenada's foreign and economic policies, in order to participate actively in national life"*
- *"Different ministers or their staff could visit schools and address students on their policies"*

— *"The Ministries should provide schools with all their plans and statistics"*

— *"Ministry of Education should get newspapers and other literature from progressive countries to supply to teachers"*

— *"Teachers should have free access to the Government Gazette"*

— *"Finance officials should hold workshops with teachers"*

— *"Newsletter on Foreign Policy should be distributed to schools"*

— *"A booklet consisting of definitions, terms and abbreviations relevant to foreign policy should be made available to teachers for the benefit of teachers and pupils"*

— *"A weekly half-hour radio programme on Grenada's foreign policy"*

— *"Teachers need to prepare themselves before implementing this"*

— *"Teachers should try to remove the shackles of colonialism from themselves before they try to help the children in that exercise"*

Sources

- Didacus Jules, *Education and Social Transformation in Grenada (1979–1983)*, University of Wisconsin–Madision, 1992.
- Rosa María Torres, *Education and Democracy in Revolutionary Grenada*, ACCESS, Vol. 5, N° 1, Reader Press Limited, Auckland, 1986.

—Rosa-Maria Torres UNICEF
Courtesy: UNICEF and UNESCO,
Education For All: Making it Work

6

The Shiksha Karmi Project

India has the second largest education system in the world. Although free and compulsory education is mandated for students aged 6 to 12, 25 per cent of children remain unschooled. Approximately 93 per cent of teachers report job dissatisfaction. Classes are overcrowded, the teaching atmosphere is rigid and classes are textbook centered. Students are receivers of information, not active participants. Although Ghandi envisioned education as *learning by doing*, India's system does not, in general, reflect that ideal.

In the 1980s, the state of Rajasthan, the second largest state in India, was a reflection of the national conditions in education. About 30 per cent of Rajasthan's population lives in remote, rural areas. Teacher absenteeism is one of the most critical problems facing the state education system.

Against this context, the *Shiksha Karmi* Project emerged as an alternative strategy to cope with teacher absenteeism and student dropout in primary education in remote rural areas through an innovative scheme that relies on the pedagogical potential and social commitment of ordinary people to help solve the educational problems of their own communities. Special teacher training and support is provided to these *Shiksha Karmis* (Hindi for "education workers"), who are trained in multigrade and child-centered methodologies.

The Silora Experience

The *Shiksha Karmi* concept was originally inspired in the work of a local NGO, the Social Work and Research Centre (SWRC). During the 1970s, in coordination with the Centre for Educational Technology (CET) in New Delhi and the National Council for Education Research and Training (NCERT), an experimental project was conducted in three public primary schools in the villages of Tilonia, Buharu and Phaloda. The project aimed at reaching school dropouts in the 6–14 year age group; introducing better teaching-learning methods, adjusted to the rural environment and to students' daily experience; increasing parental and community involvement in the education process at schools; and recruiting and training village youths as education workers. SWRC monitored these three experimental schools from 1975 to 1978.

The *Shiksha Karmi* Project was launched in Silora, Ajmer district. The simple concept of the project is the selection of two village persons in order to replace the trained, but frequently absent, primary school teacher. Provided with initial and on-the-job training and support, these two community members become responsible for teaching all the children of their village, who otherwise would not have an opportunity to get an education. Hence, they are called "education workers", not "teachers". The *Shiksha Karmis* themselves usually have only a basic formal education (up to grade 5 for women and grade 8 for men).

In the first experiment in Silora, *Shiksha Karmis* were trained during a 30-day residential course at the SWRC campus. A special syllabus and teaching materials were prepared, and the training was conducted by professionals drawn from NCERT, retired educationists, and the SWRC. Three months later, when SKs were already teaching in schools, they were given further training, this time of three weeks' duration, followed by continuous support in their work. Data in Silora indicated that student attendance increased substantially since the start of the experiment, and that it was most marked among girls and children from scheduled castes. This led to the idea of expanding the SK concept on a larger scale within the state.

Shiksha Karmi Project Expansion

In 1986 a proposal for the SK project was drafted by consultants and representatives of the government of India, the government of Rajasthan, and the Swedish International Development Authority (SIDA). The following year the project was initiated in several parts of Rajasthan.

The overall aim of the project is to revitalize and expand primary education in selected remote and culturally deprived villages in the state. Specifically, the project aims at countering teacher absenteeism in remote schools, and at increasing enrolment and reducing dropout from school, especially among girls.

Shiksha Karmi Schools

The *Shiksha Karmi's* role is to ensure minimal levels of learning for all children (ages 6 to 14) in their respective villages. Existing primary schools (grades 1 to 5) which were usually run by a single teacher are now run by a team of two SKs. Students at these schools are, for the most part, ex-dropouts. The goal is to enable them to continue their studies and re-enter the mainstream system after grade 5. SK schools use the standard state syllabuses and textbooks, but have introduced innovative teaching aids and special textbooks in Mathematics and Hindi.

Night classes and organised for working children who are unable to attend school during the day. These are also the responsibility of the *Shiksha Karmis*. Typically, students who study at night have never attended school or have remained there only for a short while. Special curricula, condensed and with a practical thrust, are being developed for working children, together with more creative and enjoyable learning environments and methodologies.

To make schools more attractive to girls. *Aangan Pathshalas* (countryard schools) have been opened and elderly women are invited to collaborate as *Mahila Sahyogi* (Woman Helper) to escort girls to schools in difficult areas and take care of the students' siblings during classes.

Training for the Shiksha Karmis

The *Shiksha Karmi* Project understood that capacity building and training for the SKs needed to be a central component in the project. This is critical not only because of the modest educational qualifications and lack of teacher training and teaching experience of the *Shiksha Karmis*, but also because they are entrusted with the mission of teaching in very difficult conditions—precariousness of the teaching-learning environment and the specific characteristics of the school clientele: poor, rural, working children, many of them with an interrupted school experience, thus requiring particular attention and renewed efforts. In fact, the key of the programme success has been the emphasis on the quality of support and encouragement provided to the *Shiksha Karmis*.

Objectives of the Training Programme

- to upgrade the initial educational qualifications of the SKs, particularly their own knowledge and understanding of Language, Mathematics and Science;
- to provide them with essential teaching knowledge and skills, and with a better understanding of the importance of making education responsive to the local environment as well as to children's and communities' needs;
- to reinforce solidarity among SKs and with parents and students in their schools;
- to give SKs personal and professional encouragement and support, through the collaborative work of resource people, local voluntary groups and government agencies.

Residential Courses and Refresher Courses

The SK candidates take an initial residential 37-day course (which was initially of a 30-day duration). This is followed by two annual refresher courses of 10 and 30 days each. Additionally, 2-day meetings are held every month to discuss and solve problems, and for individual coaching.

The initial 37-day course is designed and conducted by SANDHAN, a local NGO. Although these courses have been very useful and appreciated by SKs. concerns have been raised by some trainers that the courses have become repetitive and monotonous because they follow a single training pattern. The need for more varied and tailored-planning has thus been recognised for each specific course.

Self-Study and Oriented Study

SKs are consistently encouraged to improved their knowledge base and educational status through directed and self-study. The project subsidises the purchase of books and promotes study tours for the SKs.

Efforts to support, encourage and upgrade the competence of the *Shiksha Karmis* have included the following activities:

- participatory evaluation-cum-monitoring;
- the establishment of district/block resource units;
- field visits of block level staff;
- the publication of a monthly magazine for SKs with each issue containing correspondence lessons as well as instructions in academic and administrative matters; and
- village pre-implementation studies by SKs.

Women Shiksha Karmis—Mahila Shiksha Karmis *(MSK)*

The project concedes particular emphasis to gender issues and to the participation of girl students in day schools, women students in night schools, and women teachers as *Shiksha Karmis*.

The appointment of women teachers was initially viewed mainly as a supportive strategy to attract more girl students into schools, assuming that the presence of male teachers is an additional deterrent to the enrolment of girls. However, the presence of *Mahila* (female) *Shiksha Karmis* (MSK) in the centres has not emerged as a significant factor inducing girls' enrolment.

No women were involved as SKs in the 1984 Silora pilot project. It was not until 1986 that the MSK concept began to be developed in a systematic manner. By May 1990, 27 women had been trained as SKs. Identifying and training MSKs has evolved as a priority and a goal in itself within the project. Finding educated women in the villages and motivating them to enroll as *Shiksha Karmis* is, however, difficult. This led initially to the decision of further relaxing the educational qualification requirements for SK candidates, in order to facilitate female recruitment. It was assumed that such a measure would also entail women SKs requiring special training and support efforts as compared with men SKs.

Approximately 80 per cent of the MSKs belong to upper castes and the remaining 20 per cent (5) are scheduled caste/scheduled tribes women. Although low, this percentage must be interpreted as an achievement of the SK project, in as much as it begins to challenge two forceful walls: gender and caste.

Most MSKs are young (23 is the average age) and have heavy domestic responsibilities. Most of them face family and societal disapproval of their role as *Shiksha Karmis*, and often face the same problems with their male co-workers—male SKs. However, despite the personal conflicts that many of them have to face, MSKs claim that their teaching role has brought them personal satisfaction and a sense of freedom, as well as a stronger interest in the education of their children and, particular, of their daughters.

Training Centres for Women (MSKTC)

Special training centres have been established for MSKs in order to address the specific conditions of female candidates including the lower educational requirements expected of them and their specific needs in terms of space and time for training.

Special residential training centres have been set up for women. A three-year course was instituted whereby they would reach a level corresponding to grade 8. However, a three-year course (despite periodic vacations) proved inadequate to meet the needs of many women since it entailed long absences by the trainees from their homes. A subsequent proposal consists of shorter courses that lead to the learning equivalent of grade 5, so that they can begin to function as MSKs as soon as possible and gain further qualifications through in-service training.

Conclusions

Why did children in the *Shiksha Karmi* project achieve better learning scores than children in regular schools in literacy and numeracy, when their schools are poorly equipped, their teachers have less formal education, a much shorter teacher training course and no teaching experience when compared with their counterparts in the regular schools?

Some factors explaining such results include:

(a) the SK school is within reach;

(b) the *Shiksha Karmi* is a resident of the village and therefore accessible and accountable to the people;

(c) the training programmes were more imaginatively planned than those of the standard basic education programme; and

(d) the continuous in-service model adopted seems to have a greater potential for success.

The attitude of the *Shiksha Karmis* toward children and toward teaching is a central element. They have managed to compensate their low qualifications with enthusiasm and a strong desire to teach. Their role has given them greater prestige in their neighbourhoods and families. Through their commitment and their enthusiastic teaching, the *Shiksha Karmis* are inspiring children, parents, and the community to view the schools as positive centres of learning.

The challenge of the *Shiksha Karmi* Project is to sustain the enthusiasm for, and the involvement in, the programme on the part of all those involved: students, SKs, parents, communities, and supporting institutions. It has been proposed that permanent resource centres, in-service training programmes, continuous participatory evaluation and networking through newsletters be incorporated into the project.

Sources

- S.N. Methi and Sharada Jain, "The Shiksha Karmi Project in Rajasthan, India", in: A. Little, W. Hoppers and R. Gardner (eds.), *Beyond Jomtien: Implementing Primary Education for All*, Macmillan, London, 1994.
- Government of India, Department of Education, Ministry of Human Resource Development, *Education for All, The Indian Scene*, New Delhi, December 1993.

W.H. Taylor, *Preparing Teachers for the Universalizing of Education in India in the 1990s*, School of Education, University of Exeter, n/d.

—Rosa-Maria Torres UNICEF

Courtesy: UNICEF and UNESCO,
Education For All: Making It Work

7

The Network for Teaching Upgrading Centres

An education sector study completed in 1989/90 in the Lao Popular Democratic Republic identified teacher qualifications and competencies as a major problem in the primary school system. A high proportion of primary teachers (35% nationwide) had none or incomplete training, and some had only completed primary education themselves.

Student survival rate through the five grades was particular low in rural and remote districts of the country, and the most serious losses occurred in the first three grades, where there is a concentration of untrained and unqualified teachers. Additionally, there was no cohesive system of school supervision and inspection throughout the education system.

In order to increase enrolment, retention and quality, a greater number of schools were needed together with trained teachers to teachers to teach the early grades; a relevant curriculum; essential and attractive books, work materials, and teaching aids; and effective supervision and quality control.

Proposals put forth by the Ministry of Education (MOE) to the World Bank and the Asian Development Bank included major reforms in curriculum development, textbook production, teacher development, improvements in education planning, education management and information, and school construction. Examining its own role in identifying how best to utilise its resources to assist in Lao's education effort and to avoid overlapping of functions, UNICEF decided to concentrate its resources in the early grades of primary school and on those children who are most disadvantaged in terms of basic education.

Thus, in 1991, the Government of Lao PDR and UNICEF agreed to a five-year cooperative programme (1992–1996) on basic education which initiated a concentrated thrust of educational development in 8 rural and minority districts of 8 provinces where educational access and quality were particularly low, as revealed by a school mapping exercise conducted by UNICEF and MOE in that same year. A major feature of this programme is the *Network for Teacher Upgrading Centres* (NTUC) Project aimed at upgrading the teaching competencies of the untrained and unqualified teachers who form the majority of the teaching corps in these districts. A corollary component of this project is the *Basic Education for Rural/Minority Children* Project which aims at improving school learning conditions by ensuring that schools are equipped with basic learning materials and an environment at least moderately adequate for children to study.

The NTUC project includes the following elements:

- an in-service training system to improve the quality of teacher education of untrained/unqualified teachers in 19 rural/minority districts;
- training manuals and resource materials for trainers and trainees in the Lao language;
- a supervision and monitoring system to ensure that teacher educators and trainers perform their tasks;
- basic water and sanitation facilities provided to Teacher Upgrading Centres and improvement of the physical conditions of selected schools where the teachers work;

- linkages between the teacher upgrading centres, the schools, and the communities; and
- ownership of the project by the government.

The term *network* distinguishes the project from the more formal institutional concept of a "teacher training college", and indicates *(a)* a flexible linking of the 8 centres, each one serving a particular geographic area with its own characteristics and ethnic grouping; *(b)* cooperation and communication between the various centres; and *(c)* room for variation and flexibility in implementation to suit local conditions.

The training course consists of 24 weeks of residential work and extensive in-school exercises over a period of three years. It is supported by training modules on Foundation Studies, Applied Curriculum Studies, Advanced Studies and Supplementary Modules.

In October 1995, after four years of implementation, an evaluation of the NTUC Project was conducted. The evaluation process included a review of key documents related to the project; discussions with UNICEF staff and key MOE officials; meetings with key NGOs and partners; and field visits to three districts where the project is implemented. The evaluation aimed at assessing:

- *(a)* the overall utility and effectiveness of the strategies and complementarity of the NTUC Project in relation to the Lao Government's National Programme on Basic Education;

  (b) the usefulness and appropriateness of the training materials and methodologies and time-frame of the training programme;

  (c) the impact of the project in terms of capacity building of teacher trainers/supervisors, local supervisors, and school heads;

  (d) the impact of the project on developing classroom teaching competencies of the untrained teachers; classroom management, lesson planning, and teaching methodologies;

(e) the impact of the project on student performance: enrolment, attendance, retention, and gender gaps;

(f) the effectiveness of the supervision/pedagogical support system developed and implemented in the project;

(g) the support to school learning conditions: learning materials and supplies provided to schools, school upgrading, school water and sanitation, and community/parental mobilisation; and

(h) UNICEF-NGO cooperation strategies and effectiveness.

The evaluation aimed at arriving at recommendations for improved strategies for delivery of Basic Education for All.

The major recommendations made by the evaluation team were:

- the NTUC project should be continued with certain modifications;
- the training modules should be further revised and certain modules re-written;
- the linkages between education and health should be further encouraged; and
- the linkages between the school, parents, and the community should be further strengthened.

SALIENT CHARACTERISTICS OF THE TEACHER UPGRADING PROJECT

Goals and Objectives: The overall goal of the NTUC project is to reduce the high failure and drop-out rates of rural and ethnic minority children in primary schools in 8 project areas, through:

- reducing the proportion of untrained and unqualified teachers in primary schools in the project areas to less than 10% (by training 3,200 teachers by 1996);
- creating a team of primary teacher educators (96) with specific skills in the upgrading of untrained teachers in rural and ethnic minority areas, to conduct training in pedagogy and in the production of training materials;

- preparing and producing training manuals and resource materials in Lao language for trainers and trainees;
- upgrading the facilities of NTUCs, providing office supplies/ equipment and establishing libraries;
- upgrading selected community schools and providing basic school supplies and reading materials;
- linking community schools with in-classroom guidance and assistance with self-learning modules; and
- providing project management, administration and monitoring support.

Training Process, Content and Structure: The NTUC Project has the following features:

- *on-site teacher training:* a key feature of the project is that it trains teachers without withdrawing them from schools, linking training with immediate in-classroom application;
- *training of trainers:* trainers based at the teacher upgrading centres are trained through intensive workshops (4 weeks/ year) in the teaching of the new teacher upgrading curriculum, methods of supervision and evaluation, and aspects of community mobilisation;
- *residential summer schools and winter workshops:* these are conducted at the NTU centres during school vacations (24 weeks over 3 years);
- *distance learning study/assignments (in-school activities):* they are aimed at advancing 'students' self-learning skills between residential courses;
- *assistance with modules and in-classroom guidance:* during school terms students are visited by members of the NTU centre training team: and
- *close working relationship between trainers, school headteachers and community leaders:* the purpose is to ensure maximum support for in-classroom application of teaching methods learnt during the course.

Training Modules: The NTUC Project is structured around four core areas: Foundation Studies, Applied Curriculum, Advanced Studies, and Supplementary modules. Two Australian educationists funded by AUSAID provided technical assistance to the development of training modules, in consultation with a committee comprising ministerial level officials and teacher trainers. The consultants developed the first draft of the modules in English; these were reviewed by the committee and then translated into Lao. The first draft of the Lao version of the modules was used on a trial basis for one year. The draft modules and in-school exercises were subsequently revised based on feedback from both trainers and trainees, prior to printing.

STRUCTURE OF THE TEACHER UPGRADING COURSE

Foundation Studies

Residential School	6 weeks
In-School Exercise	4 months
Residential School	3 weeks
In-School Exercises	4 months

Applied Curriculum Studies

Residential School	6 weeks
In-School Exercises	4 months
Residential School	3 weeks
In-School Exercises	4 months

Advanced Studies

Residential School	6 weeks

CONTENTS OF TRAINING MODULES

Year 1: Foundation Studies

Pupil-Teacher Relationships

Module 1: Personal relationships

Module 2: Actions to make people feel good about themselves

Class Management and Control

Module 3:	Preventing control problems
Module 4:	Punishment and behaviour Relationship Skills
Module 5:	The pupil as an individual learner
Module 6:	Working with one pupil
Module 7:	Working with the whole class

Class Management Skills

Module 8:	The importance of time in the classroom
Module 9:	Time management skills
Module 10:	Whole class organisation; small group organisation
Module 11:	Classroom decision-making

Planning

Module 12:	How to plan; learning objectives
Module 13:	Lesson plans

Instructional Skills

Module 14:	Clear communication (1)
Module 15:	Beginning a lesson; ending a lesson
Module 16:	Questioning and responding
Module 17:	Activities which pupils do
Module 18:	Clear communication (2)
Module 19:	How to use discussion with a class

Teaching Strategies

Module 20:	Drill strategy; exposition strategy
Module 21:	Demonstration strategy; concept strategy
Module 22:	Group discussion; guided discovery

Educational Psychology

Module 23:	Stages in mental development
Module 24:	The primary school years
Module 25:	Intelligence
Module 26:	Thinking
Module 27:	Learning
Module 28:	Memory
Module 29:	Transfer and motivation

The Multi-grade school

Module 30: Strengths; organisation; the community

Year 2: Applied Curriculum

Module 1: Teaching of Primary Mathematics (Grades 1 to 5)

Module 2: Teaching of Primary Science (Grades 1 to 5)

Module 3: Teaching of Lao Language (Grades 1 to 5)

Module 4: Teaching of Social Science (Grades 1 to 5)

Module 5: Teaching of Health Education (Grades 1 to 5)

Module 6: Teaching of Physical Education (Grades 1 to 5)

Module 6: Programming

Module 7: Suggestions for Supervisors Guide and Check List

Module 8: Assessment manual

Module 9: Assessment Guide of In-school Activities

Year 3: Advanced Studies

Module 1: Physical development

Module 2: Cognitive development

Module 3: Small group organisation

Module 4: Language development

Module 5: Evaluation, testing, record keeping

Module 6: Managing pupils behaviour

Supplementary Modules

Module 1: Organisation of multi-grade school/classroom

Module 2: Teaching and organisation in the multi-grade school

Module 3: Education for girls: introduction for trainers

Module 4: The school and the community

Module 5: Principals of isolated rural schools

Module 6: Supervision; supervision notebook

Module 7: Measurement, evaluation, and progression through grades at the primary level

Module 8: Teacher Upgrading Course Evaluation Manual (for trainers/supervisors)

Other Project Components: Besides teacher training, the project ensures several materials and supplies to the schools where the teacher trainees work. During the 1994/1995 school year, 700 schools were provided with:

Textbooks: Textbooks have been provided for establishment of textbook rental schemes. New Grade 1 and Grade 2 books under the new curriculum have been supplied through the World Bank Project;

Library Book Cases and Library Books: 814 library cases with approximately 120 titles of Lao language books have been distributed for use by teachers and children;

Toshaban: Each project school has received a toshaban—a manual silk-screen printer set—provided by the Japan Sotosho Relief Committee (JSRC);

Stationary and Other Supplies: All teacher upgrading centres and target schools have received basic stationery and classroom supplies such as paper, colour pencils, alphabet charts, rulers, scissors, glue, and small blackboards;

Office Equipment: Four computers and basic office equipment/ supplies were provided to the Central Ministry to facilitate project management and implementation;

Supplies for School Upgrading and Water and Sanitation: 174 schools were provided roofing sheets and roofing nails for school repair or reconstruction; 95 schools were assisted with construction of simple water systems; and 20 schools built toilets. Parents and communities provided labour, local materials, and cash support as local contributions for school upgrading and water and sanitation activities;

Transport Equipment: The following vehicles have been provided by the project: 96 motorcycles (9 for provinces, 19 for districts, and 68 for upgrading centres) to facilitate teacher supervision; 80 bicycles for local supervisors to supervise the teachers in the satellite schools; and two vehicles to the Central Ministry for overall programme monitoring and supervision.

Cooperation with NGOs

The project has developed working links particularly with three NGOs: Church World Service (CWS), Catholic Relief Services (CRS), and Japan Sotoshu Relief Committee (JSRC), a Japanese NGO specialised in the production of teaching materials.

Funding

The NTUC Project is funded by UNICEF. Total funding in 1992–1995 was US$ 1,350,300. Supplementary funds totalling US$ 945,000 were received from AUSAID and UNICEF Australia. Supplementary funds have also been received from UNICEF Japan and Japanese NGOs such as Rissho Kosei Kai, Japan International Organisation, and Nichirenshu. UNICEF funds drawn from the Water and Sanitation (WES) Programme supported construction of school water and sanitation facilities.

Modifications Introduced to the Project

At the end of the first year of implementation, and again in 1994–1995, modifications were introduced to the NTUC project based on feedback from the trainers and field observations by MOE and UNICEF field staff:

- a school cluster system (a central school and incomplete satellite schools) was proposed in order to further promote the cross-fertilisation of ideas and sharing of experiences between the trained and untrained teachers within school clusters;
- provincial and district level education staff were incorporated to the training workshops for trainers to ensure that both levels are involved in supervising the trainers and teachers at the centres and schools;
- headteachers or senior teachers from the main schools (which are administratively responsible for satellite schools) were trained together with untrained teachers in order to introduce all of them to the new teaching methods and to

use headteachers as a crops of "local supervisors" able to strengthen school management and school supervision. These modifications responded to the recognition that *(a)* it was necessary to strengthen the school management and supervision system to a great extent than was originally anticipated in the project design, and *(b)* unless headteachers understand and share the new teaching methods themselves, they may not be supportive of the teachers in their upgrading programme;

- it was recommended that the project be expanded.

Project Achievements

The evaluation conducted in 1995 identified of following achievements of the project

Geographic Coverage: The NTUC project expanded from 8 districts in 8 provinces in 1992 to 19 districts in 9 provinces in 1995. The Project was also being implemented in a further 4 districts of 3 provinces with support from CWS and CRS.

Personnel Development: Between 1992 and 1995, the project trained 2,425 persons of which 134 were trainers/supervisors at the province, district and Teacher Upgrading Centres level; 370 were local supervisors from schools or clusters; and 1,921 were untrained teachers. By the end of the 1996/97 school year another 600 persons will have been trained. This means that by 1996, over 90% of the untrained/unqualified teachers will have benefitted from the NTUC Project.

Training Modules: Training modules were produced for the 3 year course, and for the accompanying in-school activities for the teacher upgrading programme. Based on a UNICEF/MOE review of the programme in 1994, 8 supplementary modules were produced to supplement the Advanced Curriculum.

The Applied Curriculum modules were the most favourably received, perceived by teachers as practical and immediately applicable in the classroom. Teachers particularly appreciated the modules on teaching Reading and Mathematics, as well as on learning how to select, prepare and use appropriate materials for particular lessons. Teachers found the modules dealing with child development and language development and, in general, those modules that provide theoretical or conceptual inputs (Foundation Studies), to be more difficult. The challenge thus remains to help teachers understand the whys and the "big picture of teaching and learning".

Other Learning Materials

School Books Through a Rental System: Several teachers and members of parent associations commented on the usefulness of the textbook rental scheme. In this scheme students pay 100–300 *kip* to rent textbooks for the year, which are then returned for use by the next class. On an average, textbooks are expected to last for 3-5 years. However, the World Bank-sponsored textbooks are showing signs of wear and tear, and specific measures need to be taken to protect these new books. In one school in Xieng Khouang, a teacher indicated that many children could not afford books even through the rental scheme.

Mobile Libraries: Good use was made of the mobile libraries, but more books are needed. The way in which the mobile library was shared between formal and non-formal education centres seemed efficient.

Monitoring and Supervision: A regular monitoring and supervision system had been set in place at each level. National and local supervisors provided supervisory and professional support to the teachers.

Sharing of Experiences: In most project areas, teachers (both within and outside the Project) were sharing experiences and knowledge acquired at the NTUC course for application in classroom teaching.

School Upgrading and Water and Sanitation: Of the 700 target schools, 174 had received support for reconstruction or upgrading, 95 for construction of simple water systems, and 20 have had simple toilets installed. Local contributions accounted for 40-50% of total costs. Construction and renovation costs were shared between UNICEF, MOE and the communities. In Vang Viang district, Vientiane Province, for example, UNICEF had contributed 50% of the costs, MOE 13% and communities 37%.

Parent Associations interviewed were keen to see increased quality improvement within their schools and made large commitments in terms of furniture, labour and, in some cases, the digging of wells.

Impact at Classroom Level

All members of the evaluation team felt that the NTUC Project had brought about a significant improvement in teaching methods and that the improvement was likely to continue.

The Ethos of NTUC Classrooms: All classrooms visited had pictures on the walls and learning aids were available. There was variation in the quality of the materials and their presentation; in some rooms, materials were well-selected and displayed, in others the effect was enthusiastic but jumbled. However, the overall atmosphere was welcoming and child-friendly. Handing decorations and pictures indicated teachers' attempts to make the rooms attractive. The children's conduct was lively; even in the least-developed classrooms the children were animated, interested and eager to contribute. Teachers showed considerable skill in presentation. Questions allowed children to respond with more than one-word answers, and teachers moved from entire class to individual interactions.

Classroom Organisation: The furniture in many classrooms was arranged so that the children could sit in groups to participate in practical work or discussion. In others the seating was traditional, with the children all facing the blackboard. In these classes, teachers said that the children worked in groups only occasionally and in one or two subjects. Teachers seemed clear about the reasons for seating children in groups. Where classroom organisation was more traditional, boys and girls were separated; boys in the back rows, girls at the front, "*so that they don't fight*". Groups were formed in different ways: some children simply turned round to face those behind them, others moved around the class to familiar groups. Boys and girls worked together in the groups.

Teaching and Learning: Some well-developed learning centres were observed. Teachers in Wapi, Saravane Province, said that they found the learning centre difficult to develop because of storage problems. However, in a classroom with no walls, a teacher addressed the problem by keeping her materials in a series of plastic bags hung from the rafters. Well-developed learning centres had separated areas with a learning box and other materials available. Children used them before and after school and during recess. In some places, materials were obviously well-used. There were other examples of children's interest in learning: several girls were observed reading books at recess time on the steps of a school, and children reading indoors during recess as well. Blackboards were used in non-conventional ways. For example, children were allowed to practice on the broad. One teacher encouraged children to teach each other.

Teachers identified lesson planning as an important aspect of their training. There was wide variation in the standards of lesson planning and levels of supervisory input, but lessons benefitted from prior thought and planning. Teachers in many schools had lesson plans open on their desks, and some had their supervisor's comments as well.

The Teachers: Teachers were active. They spent time moving around the room, talking to individuals as well as instructing from their desks. They showed a remarkable degree of pride and confidence in their developing professional skills. Morale was high.

Teachers believed that, as a result of their training, children understood better and learned faster and earlier, and retained their learning longer.

Teachers' comments and attitudes seemed an overwhelming endorsement of the impact of the Project and of the confidence with which teachers were putting their training into practice.

All teachers said that, with the new methods, they had to work two or three more hours per day, but none complained.

It was found that it was difficult to replace initial supplies. Teachers were using their own money or money from the parents' association.

The Children: The children endorsed the view that the project had improved their enjoyment of school and they felt that learning was easier. They did not want to go back to the old methods. The village headman of Ban Nong Nom noticed differences in the children's attitude. As well as wanting to come to school, they were more outgoing and "braver". "*They would have been much too shy to talk to a foreigner before*," he said.

Trainers, teachers and community members alike agreed that the children attended school more regularly. Visits confirmed that each class had at most three or four absentees, despite that fact that the team was visiting the schools during the rice harvesting season.

Classroom Learning Materials: Teachers made use of a variety of posters, diagrams and learning materials to support their lessons. Some children interviewed said that the illustrations were done by themselves. In terms of use of classroom learning materials there was a noticeable difference between NTUC teachers and teachers who were not part of the NTUC.

Health Education: In the NTUC Project, teachers are taught health education. The evaluation team observed a lesson on healthy eating, and parents and community members reported that the children were cleaner and washed more. However, many schools did not have clean water and latrines, an essential step towards improving children's health.

Impact on Non-NTUC Teachers: In some schools teachers not trained through NTUC had learned from their colleagues. The evaluation team was told of sharing experiences through Saturday morning in-service sessions and of teachers observing in each others' classrooms.

The Role of the Supervisors: The support of the supervisors seemed a vital aspect of the Project and provided a link between the modules taught and their implementation in the classroom.

Impact at School Level

School Environment: There seemed to be good morale in most schools the evaluation team visited. In Xieng Khouang District in a four-class, incomplete school, where none of the teachers had been trained in the course, conditions were poor, and the pupils appeared malnourished. Teacher in-service and school upgrading led to confident teachers and a better physical school environment. The process of transferring information from the NTUC teachers to others in the school added to a positive classroom climate, with willing attendance at Saturday meetings, open discussions, and genuine sharing of materials and experiences. The physical environment of the school had also been improved with the establishment of school gardens. In many cases, the classrooms of NTUC teachers were noticeably neater and more efficient than those of non-NTUC teachers.

Teacher/peer In-service Work at Schools and Across Schools: There was a consistent multiplier effect in the ways in which information gained through the project was extended to other teachers and to other schools. Saturday morning (or Friday afternoon) NTUC meetings embody an important "each one teach one" principle: to teach is to learn twice, thus ensuring better understanding of NTUC ideas by the trainees.

IMPACT AT DISTRICT LEVEL

In its visit to Vang Vieng district, the evaluation team was able to see some instances of the multiplier effect of in-service training. Sharing training and trainers covered 80% of all teachers of the district. In 1993/94, the province used its own funds to support 2 staff each from 7 districts (one district level technical staff and one school teacher) to participate in the NTUC course. After that, each district used one school as a demonstration school to apply the teaching principles, and to bring in nearby teachers to train in these principles. Of the 7 districts which attended the course, 4 had been able to use the new methods well. This demonstrated the commitment of the province and the trust in the value of the programme.

In the Palawek Project, 25 teachers (16 untrained) in 7 schools had requested 2 weeks training in production of teaching aids and use of new teaching methodologies. In Wapi District, it was noticeable that ideas were shared within a school but not across schools. It was felt that Project supervisors needed to consider better ways to disseminate ideas. The construction of materials was also not an ongoing activity in all schools. Most were made during the course. Weekly staff training did not focus on the making of practical items.

The Development of Clusters: The grouping of larger schools with satellite schools was already evident, although the reasons for such gropings appeared more likely to be administrative and economic, rather than pedagogic. In Xieng Khouang, clusters had been defined, and three additional clusters (each with about seven schools) were to be established the following year. It was planned that the core school would become a model school.

Multigrade Teaching: As the project expands to more remote areas, multigrade teaching will need to be introduced on a larger scale.

IMPACT AT THE COMMUNITY LEVEL

Parents and the community at large play an important role in the success of the NTUC project. Firstly, they are important contributors to school construction, renovation, and supplies. In many districts in the country, school construction had become an interdependent partnership among the provincial government (cement), UNICEF (roofing materials and nails), and the community (wood and labour). In one rural school in Xieng Khouang province, parents contributed for school furniture. In no area, however, was there evidence that the community and the school worked together to create a more stable and sustainable source of regular income for the school.

Secondly, involvement in school construction and maintenance gives parents and the community greater interest in, and a sense of ownership over, the school. In some cases, this seemed to have strengthened parent associations which, in some schools, were organised by parents, with parent leaders and regular meetings to discuss issues such as school finances and student problems. In Xieng Khouang, for example, some of these associations played a role with school teachers in identifying and tracking down children not enrolled in, or not attending school. In another district visited, they helped to encourage parents to take a more active interest in their children's education, such as by ensuring that they did their homework and came to school neat and clean. In at least one instance, however, association leaders were chosen for their financial status rather than for their particular interest in the school. There was little evidence, furthermore, that these associations were allowed to be involved in areas beyond financial contributions and student motivation such as school management, and the teaching-learning process.

Often, there was an active attempt by the school to enlist the support of the community by making it more aware of the nature and results of changes deriving from the NTUC Project. For example, one school in Xieng Khouang was regularly organising large meetings with the community to discuss the new methods and activities inspired by the NTUC, and parents in turn recognised its results in how their children learned in and reacted to school. Teachers thought this "advertising" was instrumental in getting parents to send children to school and in making the results visible. In the NTUC Project, teachers are also encouraged to reach out more regularly to parents, in some cases sending monthly reports of student progress and visiting parents at home to track down absent pupils.

Finally, parents also reported that children taught by NTUC teachers attended school more regularly, enjoyed school more, and learned faster and more easily.

IMPACT ON THE SCHOOL SYSTEM

The impact of NTUC has gone beyond the classroom, the Project schools, and their respective communities. It has triggered changes in the education system as a whole. Most importantly, it has begun to build individual and system-wide capacity at all levels of the system, and especially in training and supervision at the school and district level. Local supervisors (usually the head teachers of central schools) seemed to understand the Project and their role within it. Headteachers of other schools appeared to understand the value of the training and to work with the newly trained teachers in order to transmit NTUC ideas in their schools.

One reason for NTUC's success is that NTUC supervisors visit schools 20 days per month and have a mandate not only to focus on the NTUC-trained teachers but also to work with other teachers not included in the Project. This ensures that teachers are not left out of the supervisory cycle and that NTUC ideas spread through the system (e.g., "integrated" lesson plans so that teachers of the same subjects teach in a similar way). In other words, there seems to be a real professional identity arising from the NTUC among the supervisors involved. Supervisors meet regularly, exchange experiences, and receive reinforcement and enrichment.

The impact of NTUC on the school system was such that there were mechanisms in place at the local level for its further development and implementation. The current informal system of school clusters helped in this regard, allowing easy access of NTUC messages from trained teachers to other teachers, often through the informally organised Saturday morning meetings. The gradual development of more formal clusters, with clearly defined functions (both pedagogic and administrative), structures and procedures, should help even further in this regard (for example, defining clearer guidelines for the organisation of Saturday morning teacher meetings).

LINKS WITH OTHER EDUCATIONS PROJECTS, NGO AND FUNDING AGENCIES

The "Education for All by the Year 2000" initiative in Lao is supported by various agencies. Through the NTUC project, the government and UNICEF aim to bring training to rural untrained teachers. Several agencies are also working to upgrade teacher training and school curricula.

Asian Development Bank and World Bank

The Asian Development Bank, through the Teachers' Development Centre, is developing curricula and methodology for pre-service training. No formal links have been established between NTUC and the ADB-supported Project although meetings and discussions have taken place between members of both project teams. Since MOE's staff is limited, very often the same individuals are involved in the development of both projects. This does not, however, ensure communication and cross fertilisation of ideas.

The World Bank, with the Curriculum Research Centre (REIS), is developing primary school curricula and in-service training to support the introduction of new textbooks. Supervisors are being trained in assisting teachers with new methods. It is expected that many of these supervisors will be those already working with the NTUC Project. Integration is expected to take place as the new system is implemented. Collaboration at this stage, though, would ensure smoother integration later.

MOE staff feel that all projects are promoting similar styles of teaching. However, lesson planning, classroom organisation and so on are developed independently in the different projects, leading to potentially mixed messages and duplication of effort.

NGOs and Other Funding Agencies

Save the Children Fund (UK), who is involved in developing and 11+1 pre-service curriculum, has used some of the modules developed for NTUC. The NTUC Project has established informal links with the SCF (UK) programme and cooperative and continuing discussions were reported.

There are plans to use the *Ecoles sans Frontieres* newsletter to disseminate information to teachers. Channels should be set up to enable contributions from NTUC teachers.

As indicated earlier, Church World Service and Catholic Relief Service have adopted the NTUC programme, and are providing funds for its implementation in other provinces. Japan Sotoshu Relief Committee has provided school materials, including alphabet charts, child-sized blackboards and the toshaban, a portable silk screen printing system. Risho Kosei Kai (RKK), Nichirenshu (a Japanese Buddhist NGO) and the Toyota Foundation have provided some of the funds for school upgrading, learning materials in schools and training of school administrators.

Cooperation between UNICEF and NGOs is well established, probably much better than in some other countries in the region.

CONCLUSIONS

In regard to the original objectives of the NTUC Project, the 1995 evaluation found that the following had been achieved:

1. An in-service training system had been established to improve the quality of teacher education and teaching competencies of untrained/unqualified teachers currently working in rural/minority districts where education quality and effectiveness are low. Evidence consistently showed that teachers trained in the Project had gained in knowledge and skills; had high morale and motivation; used learning materials regularly and with creativity; prepared and delivered their lessons systematically; and effectively used a variety of pupil-centred approaches to teaching. They also benefitted in terms of both Ministry certification and community status.

2. The proportion of untrained/unqualified teachers in these districts had been reduced to less than 10%.

3. Over 400 primary teacher educators (local, district, and provincial supervisors) had been trained with specific skills in the upgrading of untrained/unqualified teachers. These trainers generally carried out their work with diligence and imagination.

4. Trainers had in turn trained (or are in the process of training) over 2,200 untrained teachers through residential courses and in-school exercises; over 350 such teachers had already completed their training.

5. Training manuals and resource materials for trainers and trainees had been developed in the Lao language. Experience showed that these required revision and re-writing to make them more relevant to the rural Laotian context.

6. A supervision and monitoring system had been developed to ensure that teacher educators and trainers performed their tasks, and to provide regular school-study guidance and supervision to untrained teachers after the residential

courses. There was evidence to indicate that this supervision system was well-managed.

7. Basic water and sanitation facilities had been provided to Teacher Upgrading Centres and support had been provided to improve the physical conditions of selected schools where the teachers work. Water and sanitation supplies, however, should be provided more regularly to these selected schools.

8. Linkages had been developed between the Teacher Upgrading Centres, the schools, and the communities in order to foster improved school-community partnership in the education process. Parents were supportive of the schools where the NTUC was implemented, making considerable contributions to school finances and with a high degree of interest in their children's education.

9. Ownership of the Project by the government has been established, as well as close collaboration between different levels of the education services, the UNICEF field office, the Australian National Committee for UNICEF, and AUSAID.

RECOMMENDATIONS

The evaluation report concluded that the NTUC Project should be continued by the MOE with UNICEF support. The following specific recommendations were made:

- Expand to other districts with sizeable percentages of uncertified teachers, using the human resources already developed in the Project as a catalyst for further capacity-building within the system.
- Continue selected support, through the collaboration of communities and local government, to school rehabilitation and repair.
- Select unqualified teachers for participation in the Project on the basis of certain clear criteria such as: greater

participation of females; age restrictions to include people who will continue to teach for at least five years (before retirement age); entry criteria to ensure that those people who start will complete the course successfully; and entry based on observed teaching ability.

- Reduce the residential component of the Project to two years, with some modules provided through school- and cluster-based activities.
- The training modules should be revised and re-written so as to be more grounded in the reality of the rural Laotian context and to more concretely address the nature of rural classrooms, schools and communities; consistently reflect issues and concerns related to girls' education and the status of women; be based more explicitly on methods developed within the adult education field; include information related to "Facts for Life", HIV/AIDS and other sexually transmitted diseases, and to the development of healthy and health-promoting schools. Modules on multigrade teaching should emphasise what it is and how to organise a multigrade class. Modules delivered through school—and cluster-based training should be based on appropriate methods of distance education. This revision should be conducted by experienced teachers, supervisors, and trainers working in the field, along with professionals from other teacher development projects in order to ensure complementarity with these projects.
- Continue to supply learning materials and books, to replace and add to those already provided to participating schools. Mobile libraries should introduce new books and include a list of strategies for reading.
- Review the entire system of training, support and supervision in order to encourage female participation at all levels of decision-making and implementation. A concerted attempt must be made to render the system more "women-friendly", including an evaluation of present practices to identify those which include or exclude women.

- Further strengthen and institutionalise the supervisory system (in part by including more women participants), particularly at district and local levels, through a selection process and regular training of supervisors. In order to reinforce the objectives of the Project and its implementation in schools and classrooms, the focus should be on programme and lesson planning; classroom management; the development and use of learning materials and of child-centred teaching-learning strategies; and experience exchange with special time earmarked for demonstration lessons. NTUC supervisors should follow-up on extension or spin-off effects in all districts to determine the impact and to consider whether the same supervision should also be in place for the extension of the programme.

- Identify local innovations in teaching and learning as well as in classroom and school management, and ensure their documentation and dissemination in the education system through a district newsletter.

- Develop "model" or "demonstration" schools, also termed "centres of best practice", in each district and encourage regional exchanges in Laos. Cluster core schools should be "centres of good practice".

- Further develop and refine a nationwide cluster system, with clarification of the structure, function, and staffing of school clusters, focussed on their role in the further professional development of teachers and in strengthening linkages across schools, between trained and untrained teachers, and between schools and communities.

- The linkages among the school, parents, and the community should be strengthened by more clearly defining the functions, structures, and responsibilities of parent associations, including their role both in financial support to the school and in school management and teaching and learning; and by developing community-school-teacher income generation schemes (such as school gardens, fish ponds, printing with the *toshaban*) in order to create more sustainable and regular sources of income for school activities.

- The linkages between education and health should be strengthened by developing the school as a healthy environment, through the supply of water and sanitation facilities and (perhaps subsidised) school hygiene monitors; an effective source of messages on health and healthy lifestyles; a centre for the implementation and integration of health and nutrition interventions through the organisation of parental education programmes in these fields.
- High-level attempts should be made to ensure closer collaboration and complementarity among the education development projects supported by the various international agencies—UNICEF, the Asian Development Bank (pre-service training), the World Bank (textbook development, assessment, and evaluation)—NGOs so as to ensure consistent messages and mutually supportive structures and mechanisms. This can include, for example, more frequent joint visiting of projects; increased sharing and discussion of project documentation and materials; clearer guidelines and decisions from the MOE on integrating various aspects of the projects (such as by adding girls' education issues to the pre-service programme, and ensuring a common lesson plan).
- The wider issues related to professional teacher development beyond the actual training need to be systematically addressed by the MOE. Promotions and salary increases resulting from completing the NTUC course must be promptly made available in order to maintain the enthusiasm and high morale generated by the programme. Other incentives, not necessarily financial in nature, might also be considered, including publication of interesting local innovations and rewards for innovative ideas and successes.
- As the programme expands, another system-wide issue will become important; the utilisation of trained trainers and

supervisors in districts where the NTUC will be newly introduced. This should be encouraged, with career incentives if possible, to ensure both the smooth introduction of the programme elsewhere and to rapidly develop a cadre of trained supervisors and trainers in the new districts.

- Three other important aspects of the system should be studied to ensure greater complementarity between these issues and the NTUC:
- *the assessment and examination system:* to what extent might it be reformed so as to promote, rather than hinder, the approaches and results of the NTUC?;
- *the development of new curricula and textbooks:* to what extent can NTUC ensure that its messages on curricular content and teaching methods are being reinforced by the new content being developed for the schools?; and
- *the pre-service system being developed through the Teacher Development Centre:* to what extent do the methods and content being introduced into pre-service education complement, rather than conflict with, those of the NTUC?

Source

Sheldon Shaeffer, Elaine Furniss, Valerie Emblen and Ngu Shui Meng, *Lao PDR: Evaluation of the Network for Teacher Upgrading Project*, UNICEF Vientiane, November 1995.

—Rosa-Maria Torres UNICEF

Courtesy: UNICEF and UNESCO,

Education For All: Making It Work

8

The Self-Help Action Plan for Education

The Self-Help Action Plan for Education (SHAPE), launched in 1986, is an innovation within the primary school system in Zambia. The programme covers the entire country with support from the Swedish International Development Authority (SIDA). Based on the philosophy of 'education with production' and defined as a "process-oriented programme and not a product-oriented one", SHPAE seeks to enhance the capacity of schools and colleges for self-help through the development of *resource work* and *production work.*

SHAPE's essential message is the critical importance of building a human (rather than a physical) infrastructure and network, and strengthening professional teacher development in order to achieve an improved and sustainable education system.

SHAPE believes that quality and sustainability in education are not a primarily financial problem; the most critical factor for sustainability is the effectiveness of the programme at the school level. The key thus lies in changing the attitudes of teachers, students and other educational partners, so as to develop a '*culture of innovation*' rather than to seek improvements through isolated innovations.

SHAPE is characterised by a number of key features:

- it is *integrated* within the regular school system and is related to *both Ministries of Education:* the Ministry of General Education, Youth and Sport; and the Ministry of Higher Education, Science and Technology;
- it assigns two related and mutually supportive roles to schools and colleges: to serve as *resource centres* and as *production units*;
- it is *field-based*;
- planning and management are meant to be *adaptive* and *learning-based*;
- it is intended that the programme be planned and managed by *teachers*, to facilitate professionals teacher growth and autonomy, and provide teachers an opportunity to transform schools into centres of educational experimentation;
- its organisational structure is *decentralised* and *participatory,* aimed at building partnerships at the local level among students, teachers, administrators, parents, communities, and development agencies;
- it works towards establishing an *effective network* of professional support services, linking the school with the zone, district, regional and national levels;
- its In-Service Teacher Training (INSET) model is on-site and is essentially based on *teachers' mutual professional support;* and
- *teacher colleges* are linked to SHAPE and are considered the *hubs of INSET activities* in their regions.

The overall guiding principle is the development and exercise of *self-reliance* and *resourcefulness* by teachers, schools and colleges.

Acknowledging that most of the innovations proposed by SHAPE were already being implemented by schools and individual teachers in various parts of the country, it was decided that rather what was needed was a coherent programme to encourage, institutionalise and expand such innovations within the entire system. It was decided that all resources that were made available to the programme from the Ministries of Education, from either external or internal sources, would be released only to support self-help activities and to encourage professional and institutional initiatives.

Zambia's Education System

Since Independence, in 1964, the provision of primary and junior secondary education for all children has been a permanent goal of the Zambian government. Basic education currently comprises a 9-year cycle divided into three stages: lower basic (grades 1–4); middle basic (grades 5–7); and upper basic (grades 8–9). Primary education covers the first two stages; the third stage comprises junior secondary education; and senior secondary education goes from grades 10 to 12.

Zambia has 9 provinces, 62 districts, 575 zones and 4,750 primary schools. The gross enrolment rate for the 7-13 age-group is estimated at 88 per cent and 91 per cent of grade 4 children continue into upper primary school. Repetition rates are high, especially in grades 4 and 7. The enrolment of girls in both urban and rural areas has maintained a historical trend towards parity with boys at the primary level, but a gap persists at the secondary level.

Primary schools in urban areas tend to have overcrowded classrooms, while many rural classes are under-enrolled. Most primary schools operate a double shift system at grades 1-4. In urban areas, three gifts a day are common at this level, with two shifts operating at the upper primary level. There is still a widespread shortage of teachers in many rural and urban schools, and 15 per cent of employed teachers are untrained.

The Origins of SHAPE

From 1974 to 1977 Zambia undertook an education reform that is considered the first comprehensive effort by Zambians to review their inherited education system. In line with the reform recommendations, schools-based in-service training activities were initiated in various parts of the country during the early 1980s. School-based teacher centres were established and resource activities were organised at district and school levels. Teachers were encouraged to improve themselves professionally to enable them to take a greater role in educational development and to provide schools a stronger base for self-reliance.

SHAPE emerged from these early efforts. Rather than ignoring the reforms that had been attempted in the country in the 1970s, SHAPE tried to build on those efforts. Two expatriates worked with officials from both Ministries of Education to prepare the SHAPE proposal.

HOW DOES SHAPE OPERATE?

The Structure

SHAPE operates within the Ministry of Education but in a semi-autonomous manner. It was decided not to create a separate project implementation structure. All responsibilities were thus given to staff already serving at various levels within the Ministries of Education. School headmasters and teachers served as coordinators for various SHAPE activities or resources centres. Specific appointments have been made to the post of Executive Secretary and some support staff. SHAPE has defined also new roles for conventional officers, especially inspectors.

The SHAPE structure includes a variety of institutions. The five-member *National Secretariat* has an Executive Secretary and four coordinators who are senior inspectors of schools. *Regional committees* have representatives from regional colleges and the provincial education office, and are supported by *district committees.* Finally, there are the *zone-* and *school-based teacher centre committees* that operate at the sub-district level.

Model schools identified in various districts and zones function as centres of good SHAPE practice. *Zone centre schools* are chosen on the basis of their accessibility to other schools in the zone. The human resources animating this structure comprise a large variety of *specialised teachers and coordinators. Resource teachers* are the main SHAPE coordinators at school level. *Zone coordinators*—for INSET and production work—coordinate SHAPE activities at some five or ten schools and create a network of support for teachers at the zone level.

Main Components of SHAPE

Organisational Development: Regions, districts, zones, colleges and schools are assisted in developing SHAPE coordinating committees in accordance with issued guidelines. The purpose is to establish a national infrastructure for teachers, administrators and inspectors to work together as colleagues.

Curriculum Development: Supplementary teaching and learning materials are designed and produced at various levels.

Staff development: Pre- and in-service training is provided to field staff.

Monitoring, Evaluation and Research: Coordinating committees are assisted in developing monitoring instruments and procedures for local research and evaluation.

Material Support: Committees are provided with materials and equipment, tools for production, transportation and financial support.

SHAPE Activities

SHAPE activities include:

- organising a SHAPE network involving teachers, inspectors and college tutors. Teachers, together with communities, define their needs and ideas on education;
- on-the-job training of teachers through INSET;
- curriculum planning and development for adaptation to local contexts;
- the establishing of committees or clusters at school, zone, district, regional and national level;

- training sessions to familiarise regions with SHAPE objectives, principles and methodologies;
- exploring the potential for improving on-going innovations and initiating new ones;
- informing teachers and officials of innovations carried out within and outside Zambia;
- supporting resource and production work in selected colleges, schools and districts;
- providing procedures and tools for local monitoring;
- encouraging local school committees to gather materials for SHAPE activities (tools, vehicles, equipment, books);
- creating resource centres to function as focal points for the dissemination of SHAPE ideas; and
- preparing SHAPE guidelines for schools.

Education with Production

SHAPE's concept of *education with production* underscores the integration of intellectual and manual work, of theory and practice. Productive work is regarded as both an economic tool (generating income) and as a pedagogic tool (an opportunity to apply skills and knowledge that are a part of the curriculum).

Each school is regarded as a *production* unit, and productive activities are viewed as having an economic, educational, social and cultural value. Productive activities at college level serve to demonstrate what is possible in primary schools, in terms of types of activities, technologies, organisation and management. Colleges are responsible for in-service training, curriculum development related to production, and the exchange of ideas and experiences.

All colleges and schools are likely to feature one or more production projects in agriculture, crafts or home economics. Most of the work is undertaken outside school hours and involves all students. The selection of productive activities is linked to their educational value, the availability of resources, the potential and interest of the teachers, and the needs of the school and community.

Desk repair is a specific project developed within SHAPE. It was started with the aim of resolving the problem of shortage of seating facilities, while at the same time providing new status to manual work in the school context and giving students an opportunity to take part in the repair of their own desks and to learn in the process.

In the framework of SHAPE activities, 4,000 out of Zambia's 4,750 primary schools now have economic production units and school furniture repair facilities.

Resource Work, *Resource* Teachers and *Resource* Centres

The concept of *resource work*, derived from the education reform document, refers to activities organised by teachers using local resources to improve the quality of education. These activities include an informal in-service training (INSET) and the local design and production of supplementary teaching and learning materials. Such activities take place in all school-based teacher centres and enable teachers to take the initiative in their professional development, specifically by providing them with opportunities to plan, formulate, organise and run meetings, seminars, and workshops; conduct research; and share ideas and experiences towards improving the education system.

Teachers who introduce innovations in curriculum and pedagogy and termed *resource teachers*, model and specialised teachers and SHAPE coordinations. A *resource school* is any school that implements innovations in curriculum development, materials and teaching methods.

Resource centre are of four types:

- ***National Institutions:*** such as the University of Zambia (UNZA); the Curriculum Development Centre (CDC); and the

National In-Service Training College (NISTCOL). These institutions perform an experimental function: they experiment with new materials and initiate new ideas. NISTCOL conducts advanced courses (of one year duration and above), workshops, seminars and conferences for the upgrading of different categories of personnel; it also advises and supports the regional teachers' college in their role in INSET.

- ***Regional Institutions:*** Regional teacher colleges play a vital role in the SHAPE programme. Their activities include conducting short courses for teacher upgrading; organising workshops and seminars for a variety of personnel; providing resource persons for teacher centres and resource centres; acting as centres for information and advice for all education personnel in the region; and conducting research and development work in curriculum, teaching-learning materials and methods, and school production work.

- ***District Institutions:*** District, together with school-based centres, are in charge of various activities; identifying training needs; running INSET and resource work activities; monitoring professional and production activities; undertaking research and evaluation; initiating as well as responding to needs of schools and individual teachers; holding monthly and term-based meetings, reviews, and year-end meetings; housing and organising materials to support curriculum development; facilitating teacher participation in professional support services; and offering audio-visual facilities to schools.

- ***School-level Institutions:*** Schools are viewed as places where teachers work together and meet not only for administrative reasons but for professional cooperation and exchange. A central school in each zone (5-10 schools) functions as a teacher centre for the entire zone. Zone- and school-based teacher centres provide opportunities for teachers to meet and discuss their work, identify problems and find solutions to such problems, prepare materials and produce teaching aids which are evaluated by specialists at the CDC and the university.

Any school can become a *resource centre*, if strategically located and if teachers so desire. The school-based resource centre is a room built by students and teachers, or set aside at the school, with reference books, teaching aids and a variety of objects that might be useful in the teaching-learning process. An INSET coordinator or senior teacher is in charge of this room, which is meant to be multifunctional, for use by students, teachers, school staff and community members. These rooms are often the office of the deputy-head or a senior teacher. The *resource centres* are the venue for SHAPE committee meetings, INSET training sessions, and school clusters seminars. Participants who walk from distant schools also sleep here overnight.

Schools and colleges are encouraged to undertake inter-school, inter-college, and inter-regional *study visits*, as well as visits to counterpart organisations and programmes in other African countries. The study tours aim at enabling SHAPE officers to gain experience and to identify good practices in resource and production work within and outside Zambia.

Interaction Between *Resource Work* and *Production Work*

At the core of SHAPE's philosophy is the belief that *resource work* and *production work* complement and reinforce each other: improved productivity in school or college productive work can only occur if teachers improve their skills through resource work. Conversely, production, if successful in generating finance for the school or college, can be used for professional improvement. The concept is geared towards enabling SHAPE committees to continue funding their own activities in schools and colleges so that they can be self reliant upon withdrawal of external funds.

Initially, teachers and school staff were unclear on how to integrate production and education into the curriculum. Yet, over-time, teachers, parents and students have become increasingly engaged in small-scale construction and repair activities, and have developed agricultural projects to generate income.

At this point, however, there is a noticeable emphasis on the *production* side rather than on the *pedagogical* side of the '*education with production*' philosophy, and SHAPE authorities and staff are aware of this. An important contributing factor has been the worsening economic situation and the consequent reduction in financial support to education, which has led to an overemphasis on the economic side to the detriment of the academic and pedagogic activities within schools.

SHAPE's Implementation Process

SHAPE began implementation on 1 January 1987. The first phase (1987-1989) concentrated on building a SHAPE organisation structure including schools, colleges, zones, districts and regions, through which administrators, inspectors, lecturers, teachers, students and parents could work together. The National SHAPE Secretariat was responsible for introducing SHAPE ideas and structure in every basic education school and pre-service primary teacher training college.

The first phase included:

- establishing committees at various levels;
- disseminating SHAPE, purpose and principles;
- providing regional leadership training;
- training of resource teachers in various subjects of the curriculum;
- exploring the potential for improving ongoing activities and initiating new ones;
- preparing guidelines;
- undertaking study tours to countries implementing similar programmes;
- initiating support to resource and production work in selected colleges, schools and districts.

Foreseeable problems emerged in the context of a programme that attempted to introduce new ways of thinking and operating, and new approaches to administrative and pedagogical management in the school system. The concept of equality in collective decision-making by professionals with differing status in the educational hierarchy was resisted by those in more senior positions. The zone committees, in which heads of schools were members, began to be chaired by classroom teachers who were appointed zone coordinators, and most heads found it difficult to accept such leadership. The encouraging of collective decision-making by teachers and their supervisors met with strong resistance from a traditional supervisory mentality that sees teachers as obedient and lower ranking individuals.

The appointment of coordinators in the early stages was largely *ad hoc*. Role conflicts emerged between SHAPE coordinators and senior teachers who were not given responsibilities in the SHAPE structure. At the same time, SHAPE coordinators who were also full-time teachers were overworked. The National Advisory Committee met twice during its lifespan.

Several adjustments were introduced based on problems and experiences gained during the initial stages, and on an evaluation of the programme conducted in 1993. Zone meetings are now chaired by the heads of the zone schools, and no longer by classroom teachers. The permanent secretaries of the two ministries and the University of Zambia (School of Education) became involved in policy decisions for the programme.

An important shift was introduced in strategies for the dissemination of new ideas promoted by SHAPE. Initially, the strategy involved introducing SHAPE in every school and responding to initiatives from the schools regarding material support. Evidence soon demonstrated that such strategy was in fact contributing to further inequity. In order to spread growth points evenly, it was decided that centre schools would act as satellites for the dissemination of good practice. Efforts to improve research and monitoring skills of SHAPE personnel were also intensified and guidelines prepared for that purpose.

During the second phase of the programme (1990–1993) SIDA, as the principal SHAPE donor, began to express concern about sustainability. SIDA supplied a large portion of the recurrent budget and it was unclear whether the government could take over when financial support came to an end. Thus the main organisational objectives of the second phase were:

- integrating the activities of the programme into the mainstream structures and activities of the Ministries of Education;
- beginning to transfer responsibility for some recurrent costs from SIDA to the Zambian government; and
- developing other mechanisms to ensure sustainability.

Professional Training and Development

Two years of pre-service training were considered insufficient to ensure the teacher profile required through effective resource and production work at the school level. An introduction and in-service training programme was devised that would take into account both the human side of the teacher's role and the instructional aspects of the teacher's task.

INSET OBJECTIVES

(a) Schools and Colleges

- To respond to the particular needs of individual schools or groups of schools.
- To help teachers identify professional needs and articulate these so that they can result in a programme of support at school or other level.
- To help teachers with the planning, organisation and sustained support needed for successful school-based in-service activities.

(b) Teachers and Students

- To initiate activities which encourage teachers to focus reflectively and critically upon their classroom practice.

- To respond to the concepts of goal-setting, evaluation and appraisal in relation to the whole school, the individual teacher and the child.
- To promote classroom practice which enables teachers to help children to be willing, effective and independent learners.
- To help teachers lead their students to adopt a more practical and active approach to their learning.
- To promote the use of first-hand experience as starting point for learning.
- To offer opportunities for teachers to be learners and to reflect upon the business of being a learner and upon the circumstances which support or inhibit learning.

(c) ***New Initiatives***

- To help teachers ensure that curriculum is broad, balanced, relevant and displays differentiation, progression and continuity.
- To help teachers develop a curriculum which will prepare students for the world in which they live and work when they leave schools.
- To help all teachers develop skills and strategies for the care of their students.
- To develop skills in providing cross-curricular activities within total school programmes.
- To enable teachers to develop with their students a positive attitude towards the multi-cultural nature of today's society.
- To sensitise teachers to sexist or stereotypical features in their school, in their own classrooms and in their own behaviour.
- To foster the development of curriculum leadership skills.

- To enable teachers to identify and provide for the everyday demands of children with special needs.
- To support the introduction of new curriculum areas.
- To retain teachers for the implementation of national curriculum initiatives and new examinations.
- To provide a coherent programme of activities related to the development and use of profiling and records of achievement.
- To provide training in the potential and use of new technologies in education.
- To train all teachers to meet the requirements of health.

(d) Teacher's Professional Development

- To provide opportunities for teachers to acquire further qualifications.
- To provide opportunities to develop and support leadership in schools and to foster a cooperative approach to management.
- To support teachers in the continuous development of their subject knowledge and associated teaching strategies.

In order to improve the quality of teaching and learning, SHAPE encourages the development of a cadre of *resource teachers* in all subjects. These subject resource teachers are appointed by inspectors to support curriculum development in the various subject areas. Appointments are contingent on competence and proven knowledge in their subjects, with additional training provided by the programme.

In the subsidising of regional and district seminars and workshops, priority is given to meetings of resource teachers and other key education personnel. The SHAPE Secretariat is responsible for the training of trainers and of teachers at national and regional levels, while Regional Committees organise training for district cadres.

Materials, equipment and transport and provided for regions, colleges and districts down to the zone level.

School-based training activities focus on the knowledge, skills, values and attitudes required to internalize the new approaches and methodologies at the classroom, school, and community level. Changes in teachers' attitudes and roles have had an impact on the role of inspectors, key to any sustainable school reform. The traditional inspector's role is gradually being changed to a more technical and advisory role, where inspectors collaborate with teachers more than simply control them.

MAJOR ACHIEVEMENTS

Reports on SHAPE's developments and achievements, both internal and external, agree on the innovativeness and overall positive contribution of SHAPE to sustainable education reform in Zambia, despite the country's difficult conditions and the numerous problems faced by the programme over these last few years. Such reports include an evaluation of SHAPE conducted in February-March 1993 to analyse its development and suggest eventual corrective measures for future direction of the programme. This evaluation was conducted through an examination of documents; field visits to over 40 primary schools and primary teacher training colleges, district and provincial offices in 18 districts spread over five provinces; and interviews with Ministry of Education officials, members of the SHAPE Secretariat, staff of the University of Zambia, and representatives of the Zambian National Union of Teachers (ZANUT) and international agencies.

Among SHAPE's achievements, the following have been acknowledged:

- SHAPE has created a nationwide organisational structure in all education institutions. Such structures have proved useful for developing greater professional responsibilities among teachers and encouraging local initiatives towards educational improvement.
- The zoning of schools has provided small schools with opportunities for interacting with other schools in resource and production activities.

- Teachers show enthusiasm and willingness to accept new responsibilities for the benefit of their students and schools. A formal recognition of their efforts and an endorsement of their initiatives have provided teachers and inspectors with a major incentive to remain in their work and enhance their professional development.

- Teachers' professional dependency is on the decline. There are signs of increased teacher initiative and ability to identify local resources and potential for teaching-learning purposes, as well as to identify their training needs. They have begun to develop the habit of doing things together rather than solving their problems in solution.

- Ministry of Education authorities have formally recognised the importance of teachers' contribution to educational development. SHAPE has provided an appropriate philosophy, structure and mechanisms to enable bottom-up approaches to identify and respond to teachers' needs.

- Provision of material assistance to field officers is already bearing fruit in terms of improved mobility and communication.

- There is a noticeable improvement in the interaction among teachers, tutors, inspectors, administrators and community representatives or local authorities. Teachers and parents have responded well to the financial crisis and have been active in mobilising local resources to support the education of their children. Participation in self-help projects in schools has introduced a new sense of responsibility among students, parents and teachers. A new spirit of school-community partnership is also a qualitative achievement of SHAPE.

- *Self-reliance* has become a key word in education and there is significant evidence of self-reliance at school-community level. Many institutions are able to support their own resource and production activities. Teachers, parents and students have developed greater interest in production activities in schools, partly as a result of the economic benefits these have produced for the schools, and partly because, in the current economic situation, self-employment has become increasingly attractive as a future option. For teachers, engaging in production has provided experiences that they can also apply at home to improve their personal lives.

- Study visits have proven useful. Mud desks were introduced as a result of a visit to Ethiopia, and a tailor-made course for agricultural coordinators was developed as a result of a study visit to Tanzania.
- Overall, with regard to resource work and human development, the 1993 evaluation team found that a significant number of school-based, self-help professional development and support activities were taking place at the school, zone and district level. These activities include annual or quarterly workplans; school- and zone-based seminars and workshops; the development of various kinds of resource centres; the overcoming of the isolation of schools and teachers; increased teacher initiative, self-reliance, and sense of autonomy; the development of teaching and learning materials; and a genuine sense of the need for, and the sustainability of, resource work and of professional developmental activities. In general, the evaluation team commented on the remarkable level of knowledge about, interest in, and activities supportive of SHAPE resource work.

In order to assess if and how the enhanced motivation and back-up support has led to higher-quality local resource activities and to improved classroom practice, a research committee was commissioned to undertake an assessment of learning achievement.

It would be unrealistic to expect spectacular and widespread changes in classroom relationships, practices and outcomes in such a short period of time, and considering that other critical factors that influence teaching and learning may still be absent—such as teachers' salaries and work conditions, good quality pre-service training and learning environment, and availability of the necessary materials. However, monitoring undertaken by the SHAPE Secretariat indicated that some changes had been introduced in classrooms: rote learning was giving way to a problem-solving approach; syllabus coverage was being replaced by individualised teaching and learning; and teaching for examinations was gradually giving way to teaching for competencies.

These achievements must be seen in conjunction with other efforts undertaken by the government in the field of basic education, such as support for the community building of classrooms and the massive production and distribution of free educational materials for use by the schools through the SIDA/FINNIDA-funded materials project.

Major Difficulties

SHAPE has experienced a number of limitations during its implementation. Those most often mentioned include heavy work loads for field officers, especially inspectors, who are spearheading the implementation of SHAPE; inadequate training for coordinators concerned with resource and production work; too many donor-aided and donor-driven programmes in the field competing for the same agents and schools; role conflicts among SHAPE coordinators and administrators; lack of inspectors in some districts, hampering coordination and leadership at district committee level; lack of incentives for field officers shouldering extra programme responsibilities; the severe difficulty in reaching many rural schools; frequent staff changes at various levels; friction and conflicts over the use of programme resources (such as transport).

The evaluation team mentioned the following specific problems/ challenges for resource work; limited resources, especially at the lower levels of the system; confusion over the nature, use, and criteria for the construction of resource rooms and centres; inadequate reinforcement of the basic SHAPE message; inadequate and largely uncreative use of the centres and materials developed; inadequate knowledge on the impact of SHAPE resource work; random planning and implementation of foreign training and study tours; and increased teacher awareness of gender-sensitive curricula yet to be consistently reflected in practice.

The recommendations made by the evaluation team in this regard included:

- availability of increased resources for INSET activities at school and zone level;
- a more systematic scheme for the development of resource centres and increased funds to supplement local initiative;
- professional development through SHAPE and inclusion in the SHAPE structure to be more explicitly recognised in the career structure and promotion process of the Ministry of Education;
- foreign travel to be limited to more focused and intensive study visits, with more visits organised within Zambia; and
- further clarification of SHAPE's essential messages on gender issues, with stronger training opportunities for those meant to convey it.

While important advances have been made in terms of school-community partnership for production and self-help, the challenge remains as to how to extend and enhance such partnership in critical areas such as school management, curriculum development, and learning processes and results.

SHAPE FUNDING AND SUSTAINABILITY

External Funding

Since its inception, SHAPE has largely depended on external financial resources, particularly from SIDA, which provides funds for expatriate personnel, production projects in schools and colleges, monitoring/evaluation and research, construction of resource centers, renovations in special education schools and alternations to physical facilities in pre-service college for the purpose of introducing special education, study tours, staff development, seminars/workshops, purchase and maintenance of vehicles for the programme, and materials and equipment for agricultural production, industrial arts, educational technology and home economics.

Other external agencies have provided assistance through materials support (NORAD, EC) or technical support through resource persons (British Council). Inputs by agencies in other programmes have been important parallel developments, such as FINNIDA's support to the practical subjects project, EC for the Zambia Mathematics and Science Teachers Education Project (ZAMSTEP), and the SIDA-FINNIDA sponsored Zambia Educational Materials (ZEMP).

Local Funding

The Ministries of Education provide local staff to run the programme and pay their salaries. However, most of the coordinators in the programme and inspectors who combine their duties with SHAPE activities.

Most of the funds at college and school level are generated in-house through fund raising. Production projects in schools and colleges are playing an important role in providing the funds required for various activities. Through production projects schools are contributing to fund INSET activities at district and zone levels. Transportation and food costs for teachers attending zone seminars are met by individual schools, which are also responsible for vehicle maintenance. School donations are sent to district committees which in turn forward part of the donations to regional and zone committees. At school level, local communities and individuals, including private companies, contributed labour or cash towards school construction work.

The Challenge of Indigenous Funding

Given Zambia's present economic situation, government authorities have increasingly promoted cost-sharing in education. According to some calculations, parents are currently contributing as much to primary education on a per capita basis as the government itself. Against this context, SHAPE has avoided adding an extra burden to parents and communities, by developing instead local sources of income, encouraging and enabling schools themselves to engage in production and income-generating activities. The experience of several districts shows that modest incomes from school production projects can sustain some essential work at school, zone, and district level.

At all events, it is clear that the continuation of SHAPE will depend heavily on funding from the Zambian government after the withdrawal of external funding. It its 1992 estimates of expenditure, the Ministries of Education accepted the inclusion of national counterpart funding. For this to work, the full integration of SHAPE activities into the mainstream of education is essential.

Sources

- Frank Chelu and Fred Mbulwe, "The Self-Action Plan for Education (SHAPE), Zambia", in: A. Little, W. Hoppers and R. Gardner (ed.), *Beyond Jomtien: Implementing Primary Education for All*, Macmillan Press Ltd., London, 1994.
- Benedict Faccini, "Of Copper and Fire", *Innovations Series*, N° 10, UNESCO/UNICEF, Paris, 1996.
- SHAPE, *A Report to the Ministry of Education and SIDA*, Lusaka, March 1993.
- SHAPE, *College and Schools Inset Policy on Induction of New Lecturer and Teachers and Their Professional Development*, Lusaka, n/d.

—Rosa-Maria Torres UNICEF
Courtesy: UNICEF and UNESCO,
Education For All: Making It Work

9

The Zimbabwe Integrated Teacher Education Course

ZINTEC is a four-year teacher training programme for rural primary school teacher initiated in 1981 upon Zimbabwe's Independence, ZINTEC emanated from the political will to ensure free and universal primary education despite a serious shortage of teachers for this level. ZINTEC features various important elements: starting with available resources, but planning for the continuous upgrading of teachers over time; designing a programme that includes both pre- and in-service teacher education, and combines residential and distance modalities; ensuring a salary from the beginning of the training; and offering trainees a nationally recognized standard qualification. Upon completion of training, the new teachers were bonded to government service for four years. Between 1981 and 1985, ZINTEC trained 4,600 primary school teachers. The programme continues today with some modifications.

The following is an interview with Fay Chung, first Head of ZINTEC, ex-Minister of Education of Zimbabwe, and currently Chief of UNICEF's Education Cluster. The interview was conducted by Rosa-María Torres, Senior Education Adviser at UNICEF's Education Cluster, in New York, on 8 April 1996.

Why the Name—ZINTEC?

Actually, we were going to call it the Integrated National Teacher Education Course (INTEC). But then somebody made us notice that the course would be called "*INTEC course*". Somebody suggested putting Zimbabwe in front, so it became ZINTEC.

Why *Integrated*?

Because it integrated theory with practice, college with distance education. Of course, ZINTEC also integrates the school with the community. But the main meaning was the integration of full-time residential and distance modalities in teacher training.

When did ZINTEC Emerge?

The ZINTEC concept had its roots in the liberation struggle. In the late 1970s, when we were in the refugee camps in Mozambique, we found ourselves with 3 qualified teachers and 30,000 children. We were thus faced with the situation of producing an education system that would work.

Who is *we*?

We were part of the Education Department of the Zimbabwe Africa National Union (ZANU). There were two liberation movements at that time: ZANU and ZAPU (Zimbabwe African People's Union). Both had education programmes during the same period: ZAPU operated mainly in Zambia, and ZANU operated mainly in Tanzania and Mozambique.

From the very beginning, we saw education as a very critical aspect of the liberation struggle. Of course, the 1970s was a period of military struggle so it was difficult to force education in as a main agenda.

The education programme started in 1977. Mr. Mutumbuka became head of Education in ZANU. It was partly because of his character and personality that we were able to get education in a big way in 1977 and 1978, and introduce very ambitious programmes.

We created 9 schools in Mozambique, 8 for children and 1 for adults.

ZANU had a very large contingent of university professionals. We had several highly qualified people in the Education Department, with various specializations. Many secondary and university students joined the liberation struggle. We thus had a lot of potential teacher trainees.

A couple of us did. We had two school heads who were very experienced. Mutumbuka himself has a Ph.D. in Biochemistry. I used to teach Literature at the School of Education in the University of Zambia, where we trained teachers for secondary level teaching.

The question was how to provide teacher training and at the same time provide education to the 30,000 children. We experimented with different alternatives—weekend courses, one week courses, distance education. Eventually, we came to what was the best configuration, and that was a 20 week course: after 10 weeks of full time of intensive academic study, students were put into classrooms—usually 2 or 3 to each classroom because we had an excess of candidates—to be taught for 4 weeks, then there was a week's holiday, and then they would come back for 6 more weeks. This was Teacher Education Part I.

During the period in Mozambique we trained 600 teachers with this 20-week course and we trained another group of about 20 in another course called Teacher Education Part II. We also did school administration courses for administrators and secretarial courses for the secretarial staff in the school system. We ran several education programmes including early childhood, primary, secondary, and adult education, the latter following the Freirean approach. We also developed 9 textbooks which were used in our education programmes because we could not use the existing textbooks for Language, Humanities, and History.

We taught in three languages—English, and Shona and Ndebele, the two main African language in Zimbabwe—and introduced reading materials in these three languages. Students started with English and

Shona and in grade 4 they were introduced to the second African language. After Independence, unfortunately, we were not able to maintain the three language policy. It was too difficult and too expensive.

We started in Chimoio, which was very near the border with Zimbabwe. But in 1978, after a second bombing, we had to move out of Chimoio. In 1976 the school had been bombed and many children and teachers were killed. So we went to more distant places like Tete, Gaza, and Nampula.

Around 6 or 6:30 in the morning, at sunrise, everybody had to leave. The children would meet with their teachers and they would leave the camp. Supervision was very difficult because one had to walk about two miles before one found the next class. They were all scattered. Bombings used to take place around 7:30 a.m. Because the classes were scattered, very few people died in subsequent bombings.

There was a two shift system: if one went to school in the morning one studied in the afternoon, and vice versa. All the work—building of houses, making furniture, planting vegetables—was done by the children as well.

The teacher training was conducted in one centre, originally in Chimoio. Afterwards, we transferred it to Matenji, in Teta province, to a camp called Mabvudzi.

We were mainly inspired by the need in Mozambique. In my case, I was influenced by my experience at the University of Zambia, between 1971 and 1975, where the Australian model was introduced. At Independence Zambia had 100 university graduates, so they had to take many older students. A system called "mature entry" was initiated in order to cater for working adults. I was teaching students who were 50 years old, much older than myself at that time. This is how distance education was introduced. A number of courses, particularly the core courses, were offered through correspondence. The mature age students would come for 2 years and finish the rest through correspondence.

When we started ZINTEC everybody told us we were following the Palestine model, but actually we did not know about it then. In the 1940s the Palestines had developed a teacher training programme in a similar situation—refugees, an urgent need for teachers—and had come up with similar solutions.

When we were in Mozambique we were already thinking of taking over schools in the liberated areas of Zimbabwe. We never actually did that because Independence came in 1980.

At Independence the policy was primary and secondary education for all, and anybody could go to any school. Schools were racially divided before Independence. Asians and people of mixed race—Coloreds, as they are called in Zimbabwe—had their own schools. So, when it was announced that anybody could go to any school, schools for Asians and Coloreds were empty Everyone went to the white schools.

People like Mutumbuka and myself, who had been working during the war on the side of ZANU, were unknown. People just saw us arriving in our blue jeans, taking over the Ministry, and apparently when it was announced that we were the Government, there were Ministry people who literally wept. They were very afraid of us. They saw us as terrorists, murderers, communists.

Independence happened in April, ZINTEC started operating in August, and the colleges opened in February. For the bureaucracy, the fiscal year runs from July to June, and you have to plan before February. So when we came in April and asked for money, they said we had to wait until the following July. So, UNICEF Zimbabwe gave us the office, gave us the typewriters and paid for our first two secretaries. We had to appoint the first lecturers by November so that they could start teaching in February, and here the money came from both the Carnegie and Ford Foundations.

Before Independence, black schools were mainly church schools, because the Rhodesian government felt it had no responsibility to provide education for blacks, except in cities. Cities were supposed to be white areas. Only a few blacks were allowed to live there, and these were blacks who were employed and were not allowed to bring their wives and children to live with them. In 1963 there were 5 secondary schools for blacks—who comprised 96% of the population—in the whole country. For whites—who were 4% of the population—there were about 30 or 40 secondary schools. All the other schools were run by Christian missionaries, but around 1968 the Rhodesian government decided to not allow Christian missionaries to expand education, so they passed a law which stopped Christian missionaries from establishing new schools. When we gained Independence, there was a fear that all the schools would be taken over by the new government.

Of course, we never did. What was the point of taking them over when there were so few and we needed hundreds, thousands more primary and secondary schools? What we had to control was the quality and the content, through the curriculum and teacher training. And that we controlled anyway.

As we did not have enough teachers, the idea was to plan a teacher training programme similar to the one we had developed in Mozambique. This would enable us to train 9,000 teachers while dealing with the influx of children who were expected to come in 1981.

We calculated 9,000 times 40—we estimated we would have 40 students per class. Figures showed that just before the war ended there were 800,000 children in school in Zimbabwe. We were expecting another 300,000 children to enrol, but we ended up with a million extra children. As soon as we said free primary school for all, enrolment went from 8,00,000 to 1.8 million overnight. We really should have targeted 25,000 teachers.

I was the first head of ZINTEC. We selected 12 staff from the existing teacher training colleges. Jinapah Alles, a former Director-General of Education from Sri Lanka, had been appointed just before Independence to look into the upgrading of teachers. He was a UNESCO/UNICEF appointee. Alles was the perfect candidate; he knew something that none of us knew very well: how to handle bureaucracy, a very hostile bureaucracy from the old Ministry of Education. Alles was there for the entire first year.

A British lady, Gwenda Black, had also been appointed. Alles and Black advocated totally opposite approaches to teacher training. Black's ideas was to bring all the lecturers from Britain to start the ZINTEC colleges, since we only had a few qualified and experienced lecturers in Zimbabwe. I refused. Appointing a large number of predominantly foreign staff to develop an innovative Zimbabwe-based education programme was foolish. Even though they could have been academically better than the Zimbabweans we could recruit, they would not understand the country and the people, and they would have no commitment to change. Furthermore, the programme would not be replicable in the future.

We did not have much money and we wanted to move fast. It was agreed that no buildings would be constructed for the teacher training. We spent time looking for empty buildings we could rent or renovate. If they were inadequate, we put up very cheap prefabricated buildings that came to Z $3,000 per classroom. We started in February 1981, as soon as students arrived.

The planning period went from August 1980 to February 1981, and during that period we appointed that first skeleton staff. Advertising yielded 300+ applicants, and we chose 70. Of the 300 applicants only 2 were women, so we appointed the two women. All of them were Zimbabweans. The first 12 came from teacher training colleges and eventually most of these became principals of the colleges. The 70 we recruited were university graduates teaching in secondary schools—the primary section had very few graduates.

We took over buildings in different provinces. For example, in Manicaland we found an empty school—it used to be a Roman Catholic School—that was given to us at minimal rent and eventually sold for a very nominal amount. In Harare we found an empty ex-Colored school

ZINTEC's Objectives

1. To overcome the existing shortage of teachers in order to keep abreast with educational (school) expansion in Zimbabwe.

2. To endow the Zimbabwean teacher with a sense of service to society.

3. To instill a sense of identity with the African socio-historical socialist outlook to life.

4. To develop in the student a sense of learning and teaching.

5. To develop rational thinking in students and staff.

There were many people interested in joining ZINTEC. Persons who had been working in the industry for several years decided that they really wanted to be teachers. Many would come into the ZINTEC course because it was paid, so if you had a family, it worked. We recruited a lot of these older students.

We put in a pay system for ZINTEC trainees from the minute they started to teach, after the fourth month of training. It was a really low sum (97 Zimbabwean dollars a month) but as they completed each year of teaching combined with training they got a pay increase. Upon completion, students received a full amount of $450 a month, which was the standard salary of a certified primary teacher in Zimbabwe.

The point is that while they were studying, the trainees were full-time teachers. We also had to put in a pay system from the beginning because, although they were paid, the trainees had to pay for their courses. It was a very nominal fee, but they paid every year. The only part that was free were the 4 months at the beginning and the 4 months at the end.

Anyhow, the pay system made ZINTEC the most popular course, the one every student wanted to enter. Low income families would try to get into ZINTEC rather than any other course.

I saw ZINTEC as a possibility to bring about change. When we started to recruit staff I made an arbitrary rule: nobody over 50 could be recruited, because I thought people over 50 would not welcome new ideas. We also specified a minimum of 3 years teaching experience for a lecturer, which was very low, in order to attract a younger group.

ZINTEC candidates went through an interview and had to write essays. Academic level was the main criterion. We only recruited people who had five passing grades at O level.

In the British system, O stands for Ordinary Level after 11 years of schooling. After O level, those who are going to the university would be selected for 2 further years. This is called "A" level, which stands for Advanced level. The British have abandoned this system, but many of the former colonies still keep it, and this is the case in Zimbabwe.

The first year it was a little difficult, but after that there was a surplus of people with "O" levels.

We tried to have an equal number, but we did not quite succeed. Regularly, there are 65% men and 35% women in teacher training institutions.

There was no rule about race, but most of them were black. There were a few whites, mostly older women.

One idea was clear: we wanted our teacher students to get the same university certificate as all teachers. So we made it a 4-year programme: the first 4 months and the last 4 months of the training were residential, and the rest was conducted through distance education. After the initial 16-week intensive residential course, trainees would start teaching in schools and continue to learn through distance study materials and vocation courses. After 10 terms of classroom teaching they came back for a final residential session. The whole process culminated with a final examination.

The emphasis on the initial residential course was mainly on providing a "survival kit" so that trainees could start teaching with some confidence. There was therefore less emphasis on the theoretical aspects and more on the organisation and practical aspects of education.

There were approximately 25 staff responsible for writing the distance learning materials at ZINTEC's National Centre. Distance materials were produced in modules. These modules were divided into units, and students had to do a certain number of units each week and complete 3 modules per term. They would all come together for 2 hours a week and discuss their lectures under the guidance of a ZINTEC student who became a leader during the teacher training course. Each term they had to do 3 assignments which they sent in to their district tutor for grading.

In total, 36 modules were produced. At the end the students were asked to write an assignment and to post it, at no cost to the student, to the regional centre where it was to be assessed by the field tutors.

It is true. The speed with which the modules were done resulted in very uneven quality. Some modules were just copied from books. Some of them were too theoretical. However, some of them were good and even excellent.

Initially, the Ministry asked UNESCO to provide a director, but by the time they produced names for the director we had done 12 months' work and were already on our third director. Then we asked for assistance to improve the modules, but by the time a list of people was provided to us we had already completed the 36 modules. They were revised and changed in the mid 1980s and again in the 1990s.

No. We did try and get help from the Cambridge Distance Education College. They came and conducted some one-month courses.

The distance education component was mainly print. There was a radio programme once a week, broadcast nationally. The school's radio system had daily programmes for children.

We had the main centre operating in the capital, which was responsible for producing and distributing the correspondence materials, as well as for evaluating the overall programme. Then we had 5 provincial administrative centres which looked after the training in each province (Manicaland, Mashonaland, Matabeleland, Midlands and Victoria). These centres were responsible for the submission, selection and placing of students from and into their areas. We also had three college training centres.

College lecturers were expected to become field tutors. There was a district tutor for every 30–50 students. This district tutor would visit the students during their distance education period, mark their essays, and conduct weekend and holiday courses throughout the 4 years of training. In a way, the weekly discussion sessions became a teacher training course for the whole school, and ZINTEC training modules became the teacher training modules for the entire school system.

Students were placed in groups of 3. The idea was that they would form a kind of a cluster which would support each other during the 4 years. If we isolated them, many would drop out. Also, it was easier for the district tutor to visit and follow up 3 at a time.

There were four categories of subjects: Professional Educational Foundations (including Psychology, Sociology, Philosophy, and Educational Management); Applied Education (including Arts and Crafts, Music and Homecraft), Main Subject Studies (Mathematics, Economic Science, Social Studies, and Religious Knowledge, which were studied through the distance education modules) and individual Projects (which consisted mainly of child and community observations; during term 10, students were expected to identify a main subject for study and assessment).

In a way ZINTEC had a fairly conventional teacher training curriculum because we were aiming for university recognition. We felt very strongly that if we had a course that was at a lower level, it would have a lower status and lower pay. Because of that constraint we followed a fairly conventional curriculum, much too theoretical.

We inherited the weaknesses of the old system. The old system meant that the university evaluated a teacher training college and certified it. But it allowed the college itself quite a lot of autonomy, and this often resulted in very uneven qualities. In Mozambique we had paid a lot of attention to teaching the teachers how to teach reading. In Zimbabwe colleges paid little attention to reading methodologies, a very critical area. In the ZINTEC course, as it evolved, very practical and important things ended up being treated in a very superficial way. It was partly because of the university influence: everybody was more interested in a higher academic level than on how a 6-year old child learns to read and write.

The language of training was English, although we changed the rules in 1980 which called for a passing grade in 5 subjects including a language. Previously it was 5 subjects including English. They have changed it back now. The requirement is now 5 subjects including English because it was said we let in people who were not very good in English.

Yes. The language policy we put in was mother tongue and English from grade 1. Teachers were instructed to teach literacy in the mother tongue. Only in the second term were children expected to start literacy in both languages. It also became compulsory to have one African language in the first 9 grades, so those whose mother tongue was English would have to do either Shona or Ndebele. These two national languages had to be introduced to everybody by grade 4. The minority language children therefore had to have 3 languages and the majority language children had to have 2 languages.

ZINTEC students had to do a community service project each year. Most of them did interesting programmes for the parents. Community service was a compulsory part of the ZINTEC course, but it was not evaluated.

Within the community service that they had to do, most ZINTEC trainees would do adult education. They were given some assistance. The materials were developed in 1980. Some church groups developed different materials. More innovative materials, which have to do with empowerment of the village women, were developed later.

No. And there should be one. This is something we could not deliberately bring into the course.

This came from the Mozambique days when every child was supposed to get an education and be self sufficient, be able to build a house, to make her/his own furniture, or grow her/his own food. After Independence it became official policy for every child to do this in both rural and urban areas. In fact, the evaluation of the headmaster's performance noted whether or not this was done.

In the primary school curriculum children were to grow one type of vegetable each year, and in the secondary curriculum they had some aspects of agriculture, which means one year they might rear animals, the next year they might do agriculture. In urban areas, for example, one could keep rabbits. When I was Minister of Education and visited schools, at every school I went to, however poor, everybody had taken up a collection, gone to town and bought a gift. This is a tradition. So I made a new rule which was that no gift could be given that was not made at the school. From then on I got rabbits and vegetables and crafts.

The other big programme was planting trees, which was started in 1980. For the first two years 5 million trees were planted—and 5 million trees died. People did not know how to grow trees. In 1983 we did an evaluation that confirmed this. We invested 80,000 Zimbabwe dollars in the programme, arranged for the district education officers to take a five-day course on trees run by the Forestry Commission, and organised prizes in five categories: best nursery, best wood lot for burning, fruit trees, indigenous trees, and best looking garden.

The programme continues. Since school heads are judged by the production programme, the easiest thing they can do is trees. Of course, there is no space to plant any more trees. But the problem is that heads continue to be judged by how many trees they have, rather than on how well Mathematics or Science is learned at their schools.

The university claimed that they were the best academically and also the most highly motivated. But ZINTEC training had its problems. We recruited young lecturers who had 3 or may be 5 years of teaching experience in secondary schools. They were not primary schools specialists. I think this was, and continues to be, a big weakness in ZINTEC. The Teacher Education Division has not done enough to ensure that ZINTEC lecturers utilize primary school methodologies more effectively.

ZINTEC teachers would be the most go-getting, the most organised, but they were not the best trained in terms of teaching methodology.

However, ZINTEC teachers were perceived as the best by parents and communities. During the first 4 years of Independence we allowed the parents to select their own teachers and their own heads of schools. And parents would say they wanted the ZINTEC teacher trainee to be the head of the school. We tried to explain to them that it was not possible for a student to head a school, but they would argue that the ZINTEC student was the best teacher. In my opinion, the reason they were perceived as the best teachers was because of the community service, and the fact that through their distance education and their initial training they were more in touch with new ideas. Also, they were the most motivated.

I should think the environment played a more important role than the actual training curriculum.

For 60 or 70 years, blacks had not been allowed to go to school. For many people, education was the meaning of liberation. The first day that the school opened, I saw old men weeping because their children had earlier not been allowed into the schools. That was how people felt about education: it was something they had to have. So the motivation was in the society as a whole, not resting only in the ZINTEC course.

I think it was mostly a weakness of the trainers. They were very much more conventional in the methodology than those trained in regular teacher-training, where there were primary education specialists.

That is true, but at that time many primary specialists in Zimbabwe or in Rhodesia for that matter had a more modern methodology. In a way ZINTEC moved away from what had been a breakthrough in the 1960s, which was to introduce play and creativity in the first grades.

Well, the system operates like that, but it depends on how many times you fail. Following the British system, once you are at the university they make every effort to keep you there until you graduate. If you fail two or three times you are out, but if you fail the first time you are given a second chance.

Trainees underwent central examinations every year. Exams were designed by ZINTEC, and were administered and graded by the field tutors, who also graded the distance learning modules. Final examinations were reviewed by the university.

The majority did. The dropout rate was minimal. I think the main reason for that was the clustering of three students in a group so that, even if there was a weak link in the system, the three students had recourse to the main centre: they had the lectures, they had their discussion groups every week and they had their examinations.

One of tne five provincial centres was very badly administered. I had an opportunity to visit ZINTEC trainees there and found that they were still able to get a great deal from the course they were doing, even without the district tutor.

They were very warmly received. The community service projects immediately pushed ZINTEC students into leadership roles.

In Zimbabwe there has traditionally been an antagonism between the uneducated and the educated. The educated are seen as arrogant and alienated people who despise the uneducated. ZINTEC trainees put this prejudice into question. In fact, the hostility would have directed at the teachers trained in conventional colleges.

ZINTEC trainees did not divorce themselves from the community. In Zimbabwe, as a result of the colonial heritage, when you go to college or the university you are cut off from your roots for the next three or four years, you are totally alienated from your community. Until 1991 or 1992 university graduates would refuse to work in the underdeveloped areas. We had to staff our rural schools with German and Irish teachers. Our own graduates would be posted to a remote school and they would stay one week and would then disappear. So, in 1988, when I became Minister of Education, I issued a directive that stated that we accepted teachers in January and nobody was allowed to accept another one until May. I issued that directive so that a teacher could not disappear from a rural school and appear in an urban school and be redeployed.

This situation has changed. An important factor was the return of the 300 to 400 teachers trained in Cuba. They left in 1984, spent 5 years in a university course in science subjects, and started returning home around 1990-1991. This first group of students were part of a programme started by President Mugabe and President Fidel Castro to train 400 teachers a year in science subjects. We sent many Zimbabwean lecturers there as well. We told the students they were going to have very harsh living conditions in Cuba but they would get a good education. That kind of instruction meant that we started recruiting people from the poorer classes.

Partly because of the training and partly because of the recruitment, Cuba-trained teachers immediately went to the worst schools. Cuba-trained teachers became very popular, even with the white schools and the white heads. They are seen as better science teachers, more dedicated, more hard working. This has meant a big change for the education system, because it meant that these rural schools which were staffed by Germans, Canadians or Irish, were staffed for the first time by Zimbabweans. This has also had an impact on the University of Zimbabwe, which finally has had to acknowledge the need to change.

Now it has been decided to transfer the teacher training programme to Zimbabwe. Cuban lectures will be teaching in Zimbabwe.

Before Independence we had two different curricula: a high quality British-type curriculum for whites, and a very poor curriculum for blacks, which had been developed in South Africa in the 1930s or 1940s.

The whole primary curriculum was changed in 1982-1983. One single curriculum was established for the whole country, but we allowed a lot of leeway. There was a core curriculum which was compulsory, but there was a lot of room for variation and flexibility. We allowed the old textbooks for 5 years, but publishers were told that they had to change them within that period. We also made a rule that all primary school books would be locally published. This was a big boost for the local editorial industry. In encouraged publishers to print better books and the number of publishers increased from 3 to 24, including local and overseas companies. The overseas companies also set up branches in Zimbabwe.

The two curricula were not well connected. At one stage teacher education and school curriculum development were in different divisions of the Ministry. In 1983 they were put in the same division to allow for better integration. Unfortunately, in 1988 the President decided to split the Ministry into two: primary and secondary education, and higher education. The measure was quite disastrous in terms of the required integration of teacher curriculum and student curriculum.

This was the system that applied not only to ZINTEC but to everybody trained in Zimbabwe. Teachers are supposed to serve for the same duration that they were trained.

Actually, for the teachers this did not seem to be a problem; it meant they would be in the teaching service getting full pay. This was a problem for the medical doctors because government service doctors are not well paid, while in the private sector they are highly paid.

Testing of ZINTEC students showed that they performed better in school than those graduating from the conventional college. But there are no formal evaluations of ZINTEC performance in the classroom or in relation to parents and communities.

They are mainly in rural schools and they have remained in leadership positions. Their training led them to never be divorced from their schools, never to be alienated from their environment. The fact that they had to study on their own helped them develop certain skills. ZINTEC teachers will always have an involvement with parents, and they have a greater consciousness of Zimbabwean history.

There is a big desire and demand by Zimbabwean teachers to improve their qualifications. Whether this is just a desire for the paper certificates or whether it is a real love of learning is a different matter. The fact is that in Zimbabwe there are now around 100 in-service training courses a year which are non-certificated and they are very well attended. Very often teachers have to pay to get in these courses.

It was originally thought that we would run this programme for 8 or 9 years and obtain the 9,000 trained teachers we had set as a goal. It was conceived as an accelerated teacher training programme to catch up in the early years after Independence. In fact we did not catch up—by 1986 ZINTEC had graduated just over 8,000 students—and it continues until now. The ZINTEC centre became permanent.

There were two important changes. One, it was scaled down: around 1989 or 1990 we decided to cut the size from 3 to 2 colleges; at the same time, residential training went from 4 to 8 months. This was not a demand by the students but by the lecturers, who felt that 4 months were not enough.

To some extent the entire teacher training system in the country became ZINTECized, because the students and the schools thought that ZINTEC was better.

More in-service and distance education. The regular teacher-training college has one year at college, one year in a school, and one year at college. Residential, on the job, and again residential.

We decided to reduce the number of colleges because we thought we were training too many teachers. In fact, we were not. Together, the conventional colleges and ZINTEC were training 9,000 teachers a year. We assumed we were adding 9,000 teachers a year to the previously existing teachers. But it turned out that we were not because about the same period we started losing 5,000 teachers a year.

This region is very fluid, there are no real borders; people move all the time. In Zimbabwe, for example, we have a lot of Mozambican teachers who are trained in Portuguese but they teach in our schools.

Yes and no. In the late 1980s we did a study of the pay systems in South Africa, Botswana and Zimbabwe and found that these three countries have similar pay scales. But conditions may be different. Zimbabweans, for example, are obsessed with cars: cars are a respected symbol. And it is much easier to get a car if you work in South Africa or in Botswana. In Botswana, in particular, they have schemes for teachers to get cars. In Zimbabwe you cannot get a car, whether or not you are a teacher. Young people would go and work in Namibia, where salaries are much higher than in South Africa or Botswana.

Probably a bit of both. The private sector tends to recruit from the teaching service. Instead of taking people from the university or from college they take older people who have had some work experience and good track records as teachers. All sorts of jobs that were not open to blacks before Independence are now opening up to black. So, Zimbabwe is training 5,000 and losing 5,000 teachers a year. It has become a losing game. We are training for our neighbours.

In the late 1980s it became evident that we were losing a lot of teachers. And that was about the time we started to scale down ZINTEC. Now we probably have to scale it up again.

This course is conducted by the Commonwealth of Learning with the University of Zimbabwe. The idea is to take the older teachers, particularly those in senior positions, heads and supervisors, and allow them to study for degree courses. It has apparently gone very well. We started it because of this problem of losing teachers to our neighbours. If you target a university distance education course to women and to teachers over 35, that group does not move as much as younger teachers.

Some studies have been conducted. Among the factors that make a teacher stay, availability of in-service training seems to be very attractive and will persuade a teacher to stay even if the pay is not too good. But it remains true that there is inadequate knowledge. Much more is needed.

It is likely to remain permanently. Some changes will be necessary, of course, and some have already been introduced.

I don't know if it is that special. It was special in terms of Zimbabwe, which had a very rigid and conventional teacher training system. ZINTEC broke the system, and the utilizers of the system saw ZINTEC as superior, so it placed a lot of pressure on the conventional teacher training institutions. Also, the idea of conducting 75 per cent of the course through distance education was an innovation at that time. Before Independence, the entire system was training about 300 or 400 teachers a year, while ZINTEC aimed at training 9,000.

In terms of the teacher training curriculum there was no innovation. ZINTEC used the same curriculum as the other colleges. It was decided that ZINTEC should not have a different curriculum other than the element of community service. It was innovative, however, in that it responded to the need of the time. It was sensitive to the requirements.

A "model" would mean it is perfect and this is not the case. It is a workable model. It had great success in the Zimbabwean context in terms of retention, quality and dedication of the teachers community recognition and attitude towards teachers. Those are all good aspects. At the same time there are many areas where it could have been very much more improved such as the quality of the distance education modules and the teachers training curriculum in general. This is mainly because we were trying to keep the same content and quality of the college courses so that people would not see ZINTEC as an inferior programme.

Precisely. This is where we did not innovate. We kept to the same system as before.

Some teacher trainers may have Master's degrees but they do not know about the specific situation of the schools and the teachers in the country, even if they are Zimbabweans.

Before Independence education was an elitist activity, so when it was acknowledged it was a human right, available to everyone, there was a need for total change. Ironically, in Rhodesia, before Independence, the whites had compulsory primary and secondary education for all whites. White teachers, who were used to dealing with every child having an education, were more sympathetic towards the slow learners and the children with disabilities, and were more used to dealing with parents every day. The black teacher, however, who dealt with only the top 2 or 4 per cent of the population, would have no time for less able children, no time for disabled children, and no time for parents. This was part of the legacy of colonialism. And this is the kind of change that is really needed.

I think there was a weakness in the way we recruited our staff. Defi itely the lecturers themselves needed training and self-training in terms of methodologies suitable for rural school children. As mentioned earlier, ZINTEC lecturers were recruited mainly from the secondary sector and from a system which was not very innovative. We should have had an in-service Master's degree in primary education for the lecturers while they were lecturing, or let them off for a year to do specialized courses. These were very keen, hard working, talented young people, but they were not able to work in an innovative way.

The distance education modules could have been improved from the beginning. The training of the writers and the testing of the materials was not adequate. We could have had a much closer evaluation of how the students understood the material. The only evaluation in the end was whether or not the students passed the examination.

Linking of the curriculum to the teacher training did occur but it was not enough. The training should have looked much more into the details of science teaching, instead of teaching subject matter in the abstract. The same thing with English. Teacher trainees are supposec to do between 5 and 6 hours of English a week, but they do Shak spear of Jane Eyre, instead of the practical issues that any teacher s to deal with when teaching language to small children in the classroom. How does a 6-year old child who has never heard English learn the language? What is an int resting way to do it? How should you teach 6-year olds, who have never seen a book, to read and write? These are the questions teachers need answers for. The teachers' knowledge of English as to be improved, but the whole area of innovative ways to teach English in the early grades is not being touched upon in teacher training.

The whole curriculum needs to be looked at again in terms of the types of systems, processes, and knowledge needed for a mass education system compared to an elitist one. There is still some dislocation. The curriculum was changed quite drastically so that it would cover the type of knowledge and skills that everybody needs in everyday life. But you might find that the teachers have not moved with the curriculum, despite the over 100 in-service training courses a year which teachers can enroll for. For example, Science is so new and unfamiliar to teachers that they are not really able to teach it well. Teachers now realize that they had to perform experiments every time they teach Science, but their knowledge of Science is so poor that children often learn wrong Science through these experiments. These are the dislocations that come from poor training and from a poor grasp of the topic.

ZINTEC was large in size, and this made it administratively complicated. The structure was fine, in my opinion, but again the training of human resources was weak. A person with a Ph.D may be appointed director, but he or she has never done administration before and does not know how to deal with students scattered in 100, 200 schools.

This programme, because of its nature, required very smart administrators. In this respect, ZINTEC was very uneven, with absolutely brilliant provinces and absolutely bad provinces where students had to struggle on their own.

The students passed in both cases, so if you were judging by student performance they still performed sufficiently to please the university—which marked their exams—and the district education officers and heads. But if we look at how much feedback the student had from the lecturer, there was a very uneven situation. There was students who had not been visited by the district tutor for a year or two years and who had not had a holiday or a weekend course.

Some countries prefer European and conventional standards, and would think ZINTEC is not good enough for them. However, ZINTEC is not low at all, and testing of ZINTEC students revealed that they performed better than teachers graduating from the conventional college. But of course, the notion remains that it is better to do a residential college course for 3 or 4 years than for 4 or 8 months.

What has become very popular is Zimbabwe's secondary system as well as ZIM-science. In secondary education we again deviated from our neighbours, who went for the same conventional system: boarding schools for a small proportion of the population. We refused to build boarding schools and asked communities to build the schools. If they said that wanted a secondary school, they had to do certain things: organise a committee, register the students, build the school themselves, and accept the Ministry's specifications and rules. This scheme allowed us to expand secondary education from 4 per cent to about per cent coverage. The scheme features a mixture of face-to-face and distance education.

Since we did not have enough qualified teachers, we produced education kits for several areas: science kits, woodwork kits, metalwork kits, etc. The science kit, in particular, has become very popular. Everybody has taken it and made it their own. Botswana, Namibia, Zambia, and Tanzania took the Zimbabwean Science course and adapted it. Some of them have done it better than us.

This did not happen with ZINTEC. It is not a popular model. There are no replicas of ZINTEC anywhere in Africa.

Probably United Nations agencies. We definitely did not particularly promote it.

Yes, because it is 40 per cent of the cost of the regular teacher training programmes in Zimbabwe. Of course, if you count the stipend we paid to ZINTEC trainees while they were taking the course, you might find ZINTEC has a higher cost. This has never been computed in the cost.

It is probably Zimbabwe's fault. The Ministry itself never promoted it as a model for anyone. We just did it. Also, there was no external funding to ZINTEC after the first UNICEF, Carnegie and Ford grants, so the programme was totally local and there was no need to explain to any donor what we were doing.

ZINTEC has not been properly documented and this is very disheartening. It has been a very good programme, although not without its weaknesses. It was a Zimbabwean response to a Zimbabwean problem. It was very much needed and it made an impact on the old system that was very rigid and elitist. The very fact that ZINTEC was more popular forced the old system to re-invent itself.

Additional Reference Materials

- Doreen Sibanda, *The Zimbabwe Integrated Teacher Education Course (ZINTEC)*, Education Research Unit, Bristol University School of Education", Bristol, 1982.
- Mary Anderson, *Education for All: What Are We Waiting For?*, UNICEF, New York, 1992.
- Fay Chung, *An Investigation of the Quality of Primary Education in Zimbabwe as Reflected in Classroom Teacher Competencies in a Selection of Zimbabwean Primary Schools*, Thesis presented for D. Phil. Degree, Faculty of Education, University of Zimbabwe, February 1996.

—Rosa-Maria Torres UNICEF
Courtesy: UNICEF and UNCESO,
Education For All: Making It Work

10

"Early Childhood Development: More and Better": Training Trainers in the ECD Field

"Early Childhood Development: More and Better" is a Joint Training Initiative of the Bernard van Leer Foundation, UNICEF, UNCESO and Save The Children-USA. The following description is based on descriptive documents prepared by the supporting international agencies as well as informal progress reports from participating countries. A formal evaluation of the results and impact of the initiative will be available following the third and final year. The information presented here is based on a preliminary review of the qualitative reports and observations accumulated during years one and two.

What is the Joint Training Initiative?

Eleven organisations concerned with ECD decided in 1992 to form a Coalition to strengthen the promotion of ECD as an integral component of the "expanded vision" of the *basic education* framework agreed upon in 1990 in Jomtien, Thailand, during the World Conference on "Education for All" (EFA). Capacity building was acknowledged as they key strategy to improve the quality of ECD and maximize its contribution to the EFA movement. The Joint Training Initiative emerged out of this understanding.

The "Early Childhood Development: MORE AND BETTER" Joint Training Initiative (JTI) is a three-year initiative that:

- emerged from the partnership of four international agencies committed to the well-being and the development of children: the Bernard van Leer Foundation, UNICEF, UNESCO and Save The Children—USA;
- started in selected countries in sub-Saharan Africa with a view to setting up a large-scale training programme;
- enhances the skills of existing "core" trainers in the field of early childhood development, and creates a multiplier effect by building on the knowledge and skills of those who are already trainers in ECD, rather than producing new trainers;
- stresses the need for ongoing monitoring and evaluation so that lessons learned can be applied not only to the countries involved but to other countries, and to enhance teacher training at all levels.

Some of the characteristics of the JTI are:

- it operates in nine sub-Saharan African countries: Ethiopia, Ghana, Kenya, Malawi, Mauritius, Namibia, Uganda, Zanzibar and Zimbabwe;
- the "core" trainers are selected by the countries themselves (two per country);
- an international coordinating team (the *facilitators*), consisting of representatives from each of the international partners, is responsible for the trainers' training, and their *in situ* monitoring and support throughout the three-year period;
- core trainers participate in a two-week training in year one, and a shorter course in the second and third year of the project;

- training courses are complemented with support visits to the trainers in their countries. These visits and support work are provided by the same *facilitators* who conduct the training. This ensures continuation and cohesiveness and avoids problems created by conventional training schemes where the trainers and those who do the evaluation are different individuals, often with different criteria;
- a "cascade" training strategy has been developed that operates as follows: a core group of trainers is trained by the international facilitators; each team of co-trainers is expected to train a group of 15 to 20 national trainers in their respective countries, selecting them from people working with young children and their families in education, health or community development settings.

Why Africa? The Selection of Countries

Sub-Saharan Africa was chosen as the initial focus of the JTI because of the urgent need and demand for capacity-building in Early Child Development. Initially, 11 countries were nominated by the four international partners, a number considered manageable in terms of the financing, organisation, implementation and evaluation of the programme.

The selection of countries was based on the following criteria:

- the country's commitment to participate in the three-year initiative;
- the nomination of core trainers who were experienced, ready to take on new ideas, sufficiently influential and committed to ensure the long-term success of the JTI;
- the nomination of a high-level person in a relevant government department, to support the initiative and to act as a national reference point;
- the provision of opportunities for core trainers to integrate the JTI training approach into practice by training groups of national trainers;

- the country's assurance that the JTI complemented national ECD policies and that it would contribute to future policy making and planning.

Selection of Core Trainers: Criteria for the selection of core trainers by each country were discussed with government departments and NGOs before core trainers were chosen. The criteria included:

- ability to work as a team and in a co-trainer situation;
- ability to speak and write English;
- experience of training at a level high enough to be respected in the country and possibly the region;
- policy vision;
- flexibility and ability to relate well to people at all levels.

A group of 21 trainers were selected as a result of this process (two per country; one country with three participants, and another one with 4). The profile of the trainers is as follows: 18 are women and 3 are men; ages range from late 20s to late 40s (one person is aged 60); they are carrying out a training role in their own countries. They work for a wide range of institutions including the Ministry of Education (10), Teacher Training Colleges (5), NGOs (3), Ministries other than Education (2), and UNICEF (1). This diversified background is a strength of the programme as it enhances the exchange of experiences and the quality of learning from each other.

Content: The key content areas covered in the training programme are:

- adult/child interaction;
- working with parents and the community;
- critical analysis of existing preschool curricula and parent education programmes;
- applying participatory methods to the ECD curriculum;
- preparing participatory learning materials;

- data gathering and evaluation knowledge and skills;
- participatory interaction skills;
- influencing ECD policies at the national level;
- mobilizing communities around ECD; and
- planning training for national ECD cadres.

Such content areas are key for ECD work and, however, are rarely or insufficiently covered in conventional existing ECD training.

Approach and Methodology: The teaching-learning approach adopted is *experiential* and *participatory (see box)*. This applies to the learning environment and the education methods used in the training courses, but also to the rest of activities that are implied within the JTI. A number of key principles have guided the entire programme and includes: building on strengths and experience; promoting non-hierarchical relationships; teamwork; building confidence in individuals and groups; and working in partnership.

Experiential and Participatory Learning

"The terms active and participatory refer to the trainees' behaviour in the learning situation. Instead of the trainee being a passive recipient of a one-way process of knowledge transmission, he or she becomes an active participator with the trainer in defining and designing the learning situation. The term experiential refers to a learning situation in which the trainer deliberately draws on past and present experiences of the trainee to enrich the learning process, Working together, trainer and trainee can construct situations which give the trainee first-hand experiences during the training itself. These experiences can illuminate and bring greater understanding of theoretical concepts".

Source: Torkington 1996

An important feature of the methodology is the attention given to the needs of adult learners, which includes not only trainers and trainees but parents and community members. This is particularly important considering the lack of attention of past ECD training (and teacher training in general) to the principles of adult learning.

Teamwork, an essential feature of participatory learning, is encouraged and practiced during the training courses (trainers working in small groups), and by the facilitators who work together as co-facilitators in the training courses.

The training scheme envisages a 'feedback cycle' that combines theory and practice through five stages: *(i)* starting from concrete experience; *(ii)* observing and reflecting in a supportive situation; *(iii)* forming abstract concepts; *(iv)* testing the implications of the concepts in new situations; and *(v)* feeding back to concrete experience.

Materials: Several materials have been developed under the JTI. A training manual, based on the trainers' work and comments during the first two training courses, describes in detail the training course. A training pack developed by Bernard van Leer and UNESCO has also been developed to provide trainers with additional reference material. Monitoring and evaluation instruments and guidelines for reporting on training events, for observing trainers' facilitation skills, and for assessing early childhood care-givers have been developed. Some core trainers have translated materials into their own languages and have introduced minor adaptations to suit the local culture and the needs of the trainees. Several countries have developed parent education materials for illiterate parents.

Costs: The Bernard van Leer Foundation is the major funder of all aspects of the training of the two trainers per country, including monitoring and evaluation of the entire process, the costs of the training courses and the *in situ* support. The estimated costs for training a trainer over the three-year period is US $3,500 per year. The other three international partners, UNESCO, Save the Children, and UNICEF contribute in cash or kind.

The costs of the national training courses conducted by the trainers are covered by each individual country, either by Government departments or country offices of the involved international partners.

THE TRAINING INITIATIVE IN MOTION

Training of Trainers (TOT) Courses: Two TOT courses have been conducted thus far—one in Johannesburg, South Africa in early 1995, and the second in Harare, Zimbabwe, in early 1996. The third course will be conducted in 1997 in The Hague, Headquarters of the Bernard van Leer Foundation, leading agency of the JTI. Twenty one core trainers from nine countries have attended such courses. Trainers from two countries did not participate in the second training.

The first TOT course emphasized experimental and participatory learning methods, the second TOT course was designed to *(a)* address gaps in content and method identified in the first workshop; *(b)* reflect upon and discuss training in practice issues and concerns and *(c)* plan country programmes as well as the sustainability of the JTI.

Recognizing a shortcoming of the first training course, a specific goal of the Harare TOT course was to encourage participants to be more creative in their understanding and application of participatory training methods. To achieve this goal, the JTI team tried to balance content and methods in several ways. For example, a session was introduced on 'applying experiential participatory methods to conventional areas of the ECD curriculum'. Working in groups, participants were asked to choose an area of the conventional curriculum, such as language development, and reach agreement on the learning objectives of a training session on this subject and to plan experimential participatory activities which would reach these learning objectives. Country teams were also asked in advance of the training to prepare a session using a participatory experiential method that they had carried out during the year between the two training courses. Through these activities, trainers recognized that these methods can be applied to whatever the content of the learning is and to try to encourage them to get away from a 'model' course and plan more imaginative culturally appropriate training courses.

Country Visits: All core trainers were visited in their own countries by the facilitators. Such visits have provided further guidance and confidence to the core trainers in carrying out their activities with the national trainers. In order to back up the efforts of the core trainers part of the facilitators' time in each country has been devoted to advocacy and policy dialogue with government officials and leading personnel at the institutions where trainers work.

National Training Courses: All the core trainers have carried out at least one training course for national trainers in their own countries as a direct follow-up of their own TOT courses. Various national teams have conducted more than one training course. Such training courses have also had a duration of two weeks. In some cases, the same group of trainees have attended the two courses; in other cases, each workshop has been addressed to a different set of participants.

In most instances, participants represented both government and non-governmental institutions. Participants have been very mixed also in terms of knowledge and background on ECD-related issues. In all cases, trainees lack of familiarity with participatory teaching-learning methods has been reported.

Documentation and Evaluation: Reports on general progress have been provided for each year and reports on progress in each country have been prepared. A final report of the initiative will be ready in 1997.

A primary objective of the evaluation is to assess the effects of the TOT course on participants' knowledge, skills, attitudes as well as their ability to strengthen ECD policy. An emphasis was placed on understanding the range of influences which support or hinder the core trainers' application of participatory training methods following the TOT courses. A number of instruments were created to assess the characteristics of the learners themselves as well as aspects of the local and external work environments which supported or constrained their training efforts.

In addition to the evaluation and monitoring of the JTI, evaluation methods to help trainers develop tools to monitor and evaluate the impact of their own training at the country level is an integral component of the JTI. It is hoped that several countries will also evaluate the impact of these enhanced training methods on the families and children receiving ECD services. In this regard, a prototype instrument to assess the quality of child care services has been developed.

SOME POSITIVE IMPACTS

- ***Increase in Core Trainers' Personal Confidence and Competence as Trainers***: At the first training course most of the trainers were unfamiliar with experiential participatory methods and arrived unsure of themselves and not sure what to expect. Gradually they began to relax and to contribute less tentatively. The methodology itself assists them in this direction for a number of reasons. Unlike conventional training curricula that start with theory, from the general and from what is unknown to the participants, here the training starts with the more general aspects. It builds upon and begins with the concrete and immediate experience of the participants. The course starts with a focus on the self and the group, then moves out to the child, then to the context of the child (the family and the community), and then to the wider society. This emphasizes the fact that this is an adult education situation and, although it is in the context of training of trainers in ECD, the trainers themselves are at the centre of this learning process.

At the second course there were a number of positive changes with regard to participants' physical appearance (clothes, hair styles, smiles, and the way they held themselves had changed). The pace and volume of their interventions in group and plenary work, increased. This enthusiasm was also captured in the photographs of previous national training courses which were brought by trainers to share with each other. All trainers had been very active at home. They carried out national training courses, organised and presented at meetings of policy-makers, members of Parliament, and international organisations.

During the second training course as well as the follow-up country visits it was possible to see the close and empathetic relationships which had been established in the country training teams. It is assumed that much of these changes and gains in self-esteem and confidence have resulted from the training methodology and the overall teaching-learning approach adopted by the JTI.

- ***Impact At the Country Level:*** One of the most important outcomes of the Joint Training Initiative has been the impact its participants have made on national ECD policy development. In all countries governments, NGO's, and donor agencies have become more aware of the needs of the young child and the importance of a well-trained body of professional and paraprofessionals to respond to the needs of young children and their families.
- ***Reputation and Increased Demand:*** Reputation of the JTI is spreading through Africa and beyond. Demands from countries in Africa and elsewhere to be included in the Initiative continue to increase.

SOME PROBLEMS AND CHALLENGES

- ***The Selection of Candidates and Country Teamwork:*** Participants that met the expected criteria were not easy to find. The final choice was left to the countries, and the JTI team did not interview potential candidates. Inevitably, there was wide variation in the caliber of participants, the criterion regarding the level of influence being the most ignored.

Hierarchical relationships at country level, sometimes between the team of national partners themselves—one senior and one junior trainer—contradict, in some cases, the spirit and the effective application of experiential participatory training. The terms used in national reports—'top-level trainers versus national trainers—illustrate the prevalence of the hierarchical mentality entrenched in the institutional ethos and the societal values.

- ***The Training Competence:*** A deep understanding and effective application of participatory methods in education and training does not take place overnight. There is a risk of capturing the superficial aspects but practice remains the same. The intentions expressed may not necessarily reflect reality.
- ***The Delicate Balance Between Content and Method:*** One common tendency when using participatory methods is to

overemphasize methods and to underestimate the content. In the enthusiastic support of methods one may forget the inseparability of content and method, and may ignore that the effective application of any learning method requires an analysis of the learning in all components—knowledge, skills, values and attitudes.

The delicate balancing of content and methods still challenges the JTI. During the first training course the emphasis was placed on experiencing a skills development and attitudinal change process. Issues of ECD content remained implicit rather than explicit. This was based on the assumption that the content was familiar to the participants while the method was not. However, in review of written questionnaires as well as observations of country training course, the need to provide trainees with more emphasis on content was apparent.

- ***The Cultural "Appropriateness" of Participatory Learning:*** The cultural acceptability and appropriateness of experiential participatory learning was initially challenged by participants. They have come to recognize that this method is always culturally appropriate because its knowledge base is first and foremost built on the experience of the learners, whoever they are. However, a more systemic challenge continues to confront the trainers. This training approach conflicts with the highly formal, non-participatory and hierarchical education and training methods characteristic at many institutions in their countries.

- ***Materials Development:*** One major problem has been the lack of basic materials to carry out the training activities at the national level. Large sheets of paper, felt pens, cellotape, taken for granted by facilitators in industrialized countries, have been unobtainable or in very short supply. The JTI team has looked for ways to provide these materials to at least the core trainers but the problem is more acute as the training reaches district and local levels.

- ***Support Visits:*** Visiting and monitoring nine countries has proven difficult to arrange and to carry out. The original plan included two visits per year to each country, but this has not been possible for every country.

- ***The Sustainability of the Efforts:*** The effective multiplier efforts multiplier effect of this effort depends largely on the participating countries. Financial resources to continue the training of national cadres is only one condition for such sustainability. A commitment to ECD efforts in general is essential, as well as the required support to the core trainers and the national trainers. The lack of institutional support and of an overall environment supportive of ECD activities is acknowledged by many core trainers. Lack of transport appears as a common constraint to training courses and follow-up visits. Dropout of trainees as a result of transfers to other sections or positions, is also mentioned. A report from the Namibian team suggests to include in the TOT course a discussion on "strategies on getting the supervisors more supportive". The need for a strong and ongoing advocacy effort from all sides involved—international partners, core trainers, national trainers—is critical.

In addressing this issue, the core trainers have assumed responsibility for the sustainability of the initiative following the initial three-year funding. They have formed two sub-regional groups in an effort to develop and propose a long term strategic plan..

CONCLUSION

An expected result and possible indicator of impact of the JTI on key training institutions in the participating countries is that core trainers accept, internalize and put to practice the principles and methods of experiential and participatory learning into their daily ECD training work. In as much as some of the core trainers work in institutions mainly concerned with the training of primary school teachers, the possibility of influencing the training of such teachers is viewed as essential and an important long term benefit of the initiative to a country's overall approach to educational training.

Sources

- Kate Torkington, *The Rationale of Experiential and Participatory Learning*, Working Papers in Early Childhood Development, N° 16, Bernard van Leer Foundation, The Hague, February 1996.
- Kate Torkington with Cassie Landers, *Enhancing the Skills of Early Childhood Trainers*, Training Pack, Bernard van Leer Foundation/UNESCO, Paris, 1995.

—Rosa-Maria Torres UNICEF
Courtesy: UNICEF-UNESCO,
Education For All: Making It work

11

The Shikshak Samakhya Project

The aim of the Shikshak Samakhya Project is the empowerment of the teacher. An empowered teacher can provide effective education by improving his/her teaching.

'Shikshak Samakhya' literally translates as 'Teachers' Empowerment'.

The Shikshak Samakhya Project was launched in September 1992. It is envisaged as an important part of the strategy for achieving Universal Primary Education in Madhya Pradesh.

Madhya Pradesh is the largest state in India and has a wide variety of cultural zones. It was recognised that a continuous teacher education programme, even if it is experimental, should be tried in more than one place to ensure that it could be replicated in similar areas. Therefore, five districts were selected for the initial phase of this project of teacher education: Raigarh, Jabalpur, Tikamgarh, Dhar and Raisen. There are over 23,000 primary school teachers in the five project districts.

Madhya Pradesh is one of the educationally most backward states in the country. Its overall literacy level is a mere 43.25 per cent.

Enrollment in primary school is reported to be as high as 83.86 per cent, but the dropout rate of 34 per cent (between Classes 1 and 5) considerably brings down the effective level.

The major objective of the Shikshak Samakhya Project is to develop a replicable strategy for improving the quality of primary education in the selected districts, with the aim of achieving Universal Primary Education, (UPE), throughout the state.

The project, besides enhancing the competence of the teachers, also provides for making the classroom an attractive place to be in and evolution of effective and relevant teaching learning materials and aids through a participative process.

There are some basic assumption on which the project has been designed. These are:

- All parents want their children to go to school and learn.
- Parents will send their children to school if they learn in school. Children will come to school regularly if they find the learning process enjoyable and attractive.
- Financial and non-financial incentives are poor substitutes to good and enjoyable learning in the classroom.
- The community will support the teacher and will accept the school as its own when and only when they find their children are learning well.
- India, being a poor country, has to find low cost yet high quality solutions to the problems of primary education.
- About 10 per cent of teachers will teach under any circumstances, while the large majority has to be motivated to teach. Settling of all administrative and financial claims, and ensuring promotional channels as well as openings for professional growth, will go a long way.
- Teachers will become highly motivated if they are involved in decision-making in the project activities. If they prepare their own teaching-learning materials they will in the process

discover their hidden talents as well as gain recognition from their local community.

Five critical workshops were organised in which a consensus about the basic strategy of the project was developed. Resource centres were established, each of which covers approximately. 30 primary school teachers within a range of 8 to 10 kilometres. These teachers meet once a month in their respective centres to discuss their problems, their experiences, and suggestions to make their teaching interesting. These resource centres have been provided with materials. The teachers have also been provided training and regular academic support.

In Badnawar block of Dhar district, 23 resource centres were set up, and subsequently in each of the 186 primary schools of the block, teachers began to get interested in the project. Within a year, there has been a remarkable change in the ethos of the primary schools of Badnawar. Says Sardar Singh Rathore, Head Master, Nagda, Badnawar block, "The project has helped the teachers regain their lost pride, dignity, self respect and self esteem. Not only are they enjoying their work of teaching in the classrooms but they have been able to make teaching so interesting and effective that children are eager to come to the school. The latent qualities and talent of many teachers have not only come into the open but have been widely recognised and appreciated. Seeing the children learning and longing to go to school, the parents and community have come forward to support the teacher and the school. This change of attitude has given the teachers a greater desire and has motivated them to work still harder".

The educational changes taking place in Badnawar are rapidly spreading to the other blocks of the district as well as other districts. Badnawar has demonstrated that the unachievable is easily attainable. With this achievement in Badnawar and the continuous academic and moral support of the teachers of Badnawar to all the blocks in the district, those involved are very hopeful and confident of achieving UPE in the whole district and even the entire state.

Seeing the cost-effective and rapid success of the project, the Madhya Pradesh government has recommended its adoption for all the schools of the entire state that is, some 7,70,000 schools.

Already, the Shikshak Samakshya strategy has been integrated into the district plans of 20 districts. It has taken root in many areas of the state and has created its own demand.

REFERENCE

Government of India. *Education For All: Widening Horizons.*

**Courtesy: Department of Education,
Ministry of Human Resource Development,
Government of India.**

12

The Education Volunteers: New Teachers to Take up the Challenge of Education for All

In 1995, Senegal launched a recruitment campaign for new low-cost teachers, called education volunteers. Since then, the experience has spread like wildfire in various forms throughout the West African sub-region and beyond. What justified this call for volunteers? How were they introduced? What were the expected benefits? Towards what long-term goals?

In Senegal, enrolment rates fell from 58.5 to 54.5 between 1990 and 1994, an average of one point a year. This unacceptable decline revealed the structural limits reached in widely propagating an educational model too costly for the country's resources. To maintain enrolments at previous levels, it would have been necessary to recruit around 500 additional teachers each year. However, the state was not able to provide more than 250. The number of classes closed down because the lack of teachers steadily increased, reaching nearly 2,000 in 1994. In conditions like these, stagnation or even worse decline, seemed inevitable. This was unacceptable for several reasons. It would have meant denying education to one child out of two, condemning at least half of the country's citizenery to illiteracy in the 21st century, handicapping the national potential for development and nurturing the vicious circle of ignorance/poverty. Thus the state was obliged to do something to reverse this trend.

Promoting Equity and General Interest

Indeed, universal access to education, or education for all, must be an imperative on the ethical level and a *sine qua non* for sustainable development in all countries. Consequently, this objective becomes an obligation which pushes political choices in *two* directions. The *first* consists in significantly increasing the resources earmarked for education. Senegal with 33 per cent of the state budget, namely 4.2 per cent of the PNB, destined for education, no longer had a significant margin in this direction. It was thus necessary, in addition to increasing resources, to make efficiency gains in the way resources were being used. The student/teacher ratio (59/1) had already reached its limits, with overcrowded classrooms and a widespread use of double-shift classes and multi-grade classroom solutions for over 30 per cent of enrolments. Reducing repetition and the number of drop-outs, linked to the improvement of the quality of learning, meant major educational expenses, while at the same time postponing hoped-for benefits to the long term. Finally, analysis revealed that teacher costs swallowed up more than 90 per cent of public budgets per student at the primary school level. The reduction of the wage bill, therefore, constituted the second and most promising option in view of opening the school doors to hundreds of thousands of children, mostly from the poorest sectors of society, while creating possibilities for investing in other quality factors (teaching materials, training, supervision, etc.). Such a trade-off was not easy, either politically or socially. However, by balancing the risks involved against those caused by the decline of enrolments, the general interest and the principle of equity weighed heavily in favour of an initiative whose benefits were numerous and reach was widespread. The rest was a question of political will.

Training Enough Teachers and Ensuring Quality

Lessons drawn from earlier experiences made it possible to develop a volunteer teachers project on a new basis:

- to place the project beyond the rigid constraints of the civil service, especially the relationship between a diploma and the pay index, so as to recruit the maximum (1,500 beyond the 500 recruited each year, i.e. four times the usual number);
- to avoid recruiting underqualified teachers solely to keep the wage bill down, by demanding from candidates a minimum academic (high school diploma) and professional qualifications (4 months' initial training in classroom skills) to teach at primary level;
- to organise an objective and transparent screening process so as to recruit the best candidates;
- to place volunteers in rural areas and regions with urgent needs through an equitable allotment of recruitment quotas and by shifting recruitment and management as much as possible to district (Department) levels;
- to combine a call to young graduates for social voluntary work with the realities of the workplace in determining pay levels (twice the GDP per capita, i.e. three times less than the average cost of a government teacher) in keeping with the enrolment objectives and acceptable living conditions for a young, unmarried volunteer in a rural environment (criteria set according to age, marital status, and previous experience);
- to limit the time of voluntary services to a reasonable period, while assuring continuity (two-year contract, renewable only once);
- at the same time, to open up possibilities for the volunteers to enter into regular teaching positions once the volunteer period is over;
- to provide motivational support to the volunteer (free housing offered by the community and a budget for in-service teacher training, both at a distance and on location).

It is with these goals and means in mind that the project was set up in 1995, and is still continuing.

Encouraging Results

For 1,500 new positions, the first competition registered 32,000 candidates. Five years later, the trend continues, and recently, it was decided to increase the number of positions open to recruitment.

As for access to education, the decline in enrolments has been stopped. Better still, the enrolment rates have increased from 54.5 to 68.3 between 1995 and 1999. As for gender equity, the parity index between girls and boys has substantially moved towards equality (from 0.72 to 0.88) while the gap between the regions with the highest and lowest rates of enrolments has been reduced by 15 points. An encouraging example in this sense is the region of Tamba whose enrolment rates have increased from 40 to 71 during this same period.

However, what about quality? Contrary to fears expressed, no negative impact on the available quality indicators was noted. Between 1994 and 1999, the dropout rate was steady at about 6 per cent, repeated classes were reduced from 16 to 14 per cent, and graduation figures grew from 21.9 to 41.25 per cent. Although it is impossible to establish a causal link between relative quality improvements and the volunteer project, one can at least note that the latter contributed to substantially lowering the student/teacher ratio (from 59/1 to 49/1), thus making classes less congested. Moreover, the performance of volunteers at professional examinations (to upgrade teacher training certificates) was significantly higher than that of tenured teachers. This is understandable, since the level of education of the former is higher (over 73% of volunteers had a high-school certificate and above on their initial recruitment). Finally, these indications confirm the testimony gathered by external evaluation teams from communities, principals and school inspectors who unanimously expressed their satisfaction with the quality of services provided by volunteers.

Controversies, Problems and Challenges

All the same the opponents of the project continue to pepper it with criticisms on issues such as the low esteem and increased precariousness of the teaching profession with the obvious consequences: demotivation among teachers, diversion of the best students from teaching, the instability of volunteers, the low quality of education, etc. Beyond these concerns, it would be proper to examine the real problems which arise from a cohabitation between various categories of teachers doing the same job and receiving unequal remuneration. Evidently, this is a cause of frustration and potentially a source of rebellion, which makes the benefits at all times vulnerable and poses a real challenge to management. One of the responses was to develop an open and ongoing dialogue to broaden understanding and support among the key players. Since consensus was hard to achieve, given the sectional claims at stake, the communications policy was intensified in the media and public meetings by confronting the various positions so as to arrive at a compromise in terms of public opinion. Thus, what occurred was a settling of grievances and particular interests which underlined some major challenges and real problems. The third response was to set up a monitoring and evaluation apparatus. This made it possible to detect in time difficulties that were arising irregularities in selection or implementation of service, delays in payment of salaries, strikes, resignations, etc.) so as to provide immediate solutions, while at the same time setting up flexible mechanisms for prevention and corrective action.

Necessary Changes and New Perspectives

Beyond these adjustment strategies, real changes are necessary. The transition from the cohabitation of various teaching categories towards a harmonization of roles and statuses requires careful incremental adjustments. They can be achieved through compromises that must be found between the legitimate aspirations of volunteers to benefit from the same treatment as their civil service colleagues and the budget constraints which necessitated recourse to this kind of recruitment in the first place. The solution chosen in Senegal was to create an intermediate body of contractual teachers to absorb volunteers at the end of their contract by offering them a 25 per cent pay rise, an indeterminate contract and a career plan. In order not to perpetuate unfair treatment, recruitment methods for all teachers were revised so as to give henceforth exclusive access to former volunteers who had become contractual teachers. Pushing this approach further, some countries foresee promoting experienced teachers into pedagogical support and supervisory functions (educational counsellors or principals) access to which is gained through experience and merit. This would justify the difference in salaries.

Such changes could guarantee the management and financial sustainability of these types of recruitment methods which aim to accelerate the attainment of education for all. However, why should teachers alone bear the full brunt of the sacrifice? Why does the reform not affect other sectors of the civil service? Why cannot other stakeholders in society also be made to contribute? This offers wide scope for enquiry, negotiation and reform by the governments concerned and their education partners.

Source: *IIEP News Letter Vol. XIX, No. 2, April-June 2001*, pp: 9–10 (Published by International Institute of Educational Planning, UNESCO, Paris).

—Mamador Ndoye
Co-ordinator of the U.N.
Special Initiative for Africa, World Bank.

13

Short-Term Teacher Training Programme

Education, as the centerpiece of human resources development in the overall paradigm of development, has not secured national priority. There is national commitment at the highest levels among policy makers, educationists, community and all concerned persons that education is the key to balanced socio-economic development.

Development of Education in India 1993-94,
Dept. of Education, MHRD, Govt. of India.

Introduction

The attempt to place the human being at the centre of development has brought into sharp focus the urgent need to make education a reality for every citizen of India. Therefore, while the nation's constitution commits to provide free and compulsory education to all children upto the age of fourteen, education policy is constantly being reviewed in order to extend opportunities for learning to all those—children and adults—who account for India's 320.41 million illiterate people; policy makers of India have been acutely aware that such statistics represent only the larger canvas, subsumed within which are linguistic, cultural, socio-economic and geographic complexities that require sensitive handling. The human angle of problems related to education can no longer be ignored in a world that in now demanding that every citizen enjoys equally the fruits of development.

India reacted with great determination to the pledges made at the Education for All Summit in Delhi, and as a part of the follow up organised a conference of Chief Ministers in February 1994, and the Chief Ministers expressed complete unanimity at awarding high national priority to Education For All (EFA) and placing EFA at the centre of India's development agenda and also reaffirmed that—highest priority would be given to primary and adult education, major efforts would be made to mobilise resources for education, optimal utilisation of resources would be ensured, outlay for education, would be increased from 3.7% to 6% GNP, special attention would be focussed on seven high population, low literacy states which account for more than 70% of India's illiterate people, and a spirit of democratic decentralization and community participation would become the basis for education development.

Basic education is more than an end in itself. It is the formulation for life long learning and human development on which countries may be build, systematically, further levels and types of education and training.

Identifying the role of education in human life, Article 7 of the 'World Declaration on Education For All Meeting Basic Learning Needs' states that national, regional and local educational authorities have a. unique obligation to provide basic education for all, but they can not be expected to supply every human, financial or organisational requirement for this task. New and revitalised partnerships at all levels will be necessary: partnerships among all sub-sectors and forms of education, recognising the special role of teachers and that of administrators and other educational personnel; partnerships between education and other government departments, including planning, finance, labour, communication, and other social sectors, partnerships between government and non-government organisations, the private sector, local communities, religious groups, and families. The recognition of the vital role of both families and teachers is particularly important.

Quality of education and even retention are obviously affected by the availability of essential inputs: teachers with necessary training and skills, learning materials of interest and quality, and adequate buildings and equipment—as envisaged in the Framework for Action of the Delhi Declaration.

The role of teacher as also said in the Framework for Action of the Delhi Declaration, is central in basic education. Nearly all issues, whether related to goals, learning achievements, organisation of programmes or performance of the education system, involve an analysis of the role of teachers: their behaviours, performance, remuneration, incentives, skills and how they are used in the system. In particular, the traditional teacher recruitment and preparation model has to be re-examined in the light of the central goal of basic education, teaching essential learning and life skills.

The Delhi Declaration stress that we will improve the quality and relevance of basic education programmes by intensifying the efforts to improve the status, training and conditions of teachers, to improve learning contents and material and to carry out other necessary reforms of our education system; and there is also a point in the Framework of Action of the EFA emphasising the role of teachers that the pre-eminent role of teachers as well as other educational personnel in providing quality basic education needs to be recognised and developed to optimise their contribution.

The government can alone not do all the necessary for the promotion of education and its various components. The private sector and the voluntary agencies have a legitimate role to place in the field of education. On this, the Recommendation 2 (b) of the Report of the National Advisory Committee (Yash Pal Committee) states that the voluntary organisations with a specific commitment to pedagogical innovations within the formal and non-formal system be provided greater freedom and support in development of curriculum, text books and teacher training; and this has been endorsed by the Report of the Group to Examine the Feasibility of implementing the Recommendations of the National Advisory Committee set up to suggest ways to Reduce Academic Burden by stating that the Group fully agrees that voluntary organisations with a commitment to education should be encouraged in all possible manners. The Group also noted that the governments, both at the national and the state levels, have, in recent past, made substantial move to expand such cooperation. The process need to be continued.

Let the education be for all and all for education. All the necessary steps to make India a total literate nation are to be taken without any delay and within all possible ways.

Need for Short-Term Teacher Training

In any or every educational system, the teacher is the crucial persons to play all roles in educating the respondents. If the teacher is an untrained, un-skilled and un-interested one, the whole educational system in her/his set-up will collapse unnoticingly and the people attending to it will be spoiled and or damages, at sometimes, beyond repair, and if the teacher is a trained, skilled and committed one, the whole educational system in her/his set-up will produce quality education and enlightened citizens which contribute for the development and progress of the nation.

Identifying the role of teacher and his place in education, the Government of India has introduced nation-wide orientation programmes such as Mass Teacher Orientation Programme (MTOP), Programme of Mass Orientation for School Teacher (PMOST), Special Orientation for School Teacher (SOPT), etc. at national level and is supporting the state level programmes such as Andhra Pradesh Primary Education Project in A.P., Shiksha Karmi Project in Rajasthan, Shishak Samakhya Project in M.P., etc. The Operation Blackboard (OB), the District Primary Education Programme (DPEP), the National Literacy

Mission (NLM), the Total Literacy Campaigns (TLCs), the Bihar Education Project (BEP), the Mahila Samakhya Programmes (*MSc*), the Lok Jumbish Project (LJ), the Uttar Pradesh Primary Education Project (UPPEP), etc., have also had a component on teacher improvement. All these programmes highlight the role of teachers in the system of education and nation building.

Nearly one thirds of the schools in India are managed by private organisations and associations. Though the private managements are contributing for the cause of education, they are not in a position to appoint the trained teachers in their schools because of the acute shortage of trained teachers. Moreover, the under-graduates, the women, the house-wives, etc., usually work in these private institutions and these are also preferred by the private managements as these stay for a long time and term in the schools and also work with minimum salaries as they lack any qualitative skills in teaching.

But, the education provided either in government schools or in private schools must be a qualitative one, must inculcate interest in learners, must reduce the drop-out rate, must imbibe the Minimum Levels of Learning and above all must make the students continue education upto the expected levels. For this, the teachers need proper training—full length or abridged.

The facilities to train teachers is meagre in India and the trained teachers too prefer to work in government schools or government aided schools for want of good salaries and service conditions. Though the demand for teachers is more both in government schools and in private schools, the Governments are not granting permission to start new teacher training institutions because of various reasons.

At this juncture, the only alternative is to provide short-term training to the untrained teachers who are working in schools and who are interested in teaching profession in order to make them skillful in effective teaching. The short-term teacher training given to these untrained teachers or candidates interested in teaching will help them in understanding the philosophy of teacher education, in using proper teaching methodologies, in assessing the student personality and helping in all-round development, in using appropriate teaching aids, in presenting the content systematically, in implementing the MLL approach, in making the children participate in pleasant learning, in arranging a lively class room, etc. As the teacher is the soul of education, the child is the heart of education and the infrastructural facilities are the body of education, let all contribute for the promotion of teaching skills and educational facilities.

Components of Short-term Teacher Training Programme

The course work of the Short-Term Teacher Training Programme will be for 30 days having 210 credit hours including both theory and practicals. The course includes the subjects, viz., Teacher and Education, Educational Psychology, Perspectives of Education Teaching Methodology, Educational Technology, and Practical work.

1. ***Teacher and Education:*** Education and Philosophy, Agencies of Education, Theories of Education, Education and Sociology, Education and Culture, Education and Religion, Education and Democracy, Education and Economics, Education and Science, National Integration, and International Understanding.

2. ***Educational Psychology:*** Psychology, Educational Psychology, Human Growth and Development, Human Needs, Perception, Learning, Thinking, Memory, Intelligence Personality, Adjustment, Discipline, Creativity, Mental Health, Guidance and Counselling.

3. ***Perspectives of Education:*** Stages of Education—Pre-Primary, Secondary and Higher Education, Vocationalisation of Education, Management Education, Teacher Education, Special Education, Population Education, Social/Adult Education, Life-long Education, Value Education, Women Education, Socially Useful Productive Work, Universalization Elementary Education, Equalisation of Educational

Opportunities, Minimum Levels of Learning, New Projects and Programmes in Education, Quality Plus Equality.

4. ***Educational Technology:*** Educational Technology, Audio Visual Teaching Aids, Display Boards, Graphic Aids, Three-Dimensional Aids, Projects Aids, Audio-Video Aids, Co-curricular Programmes, Improvised Teaching Aids.

5. ***Teaching Methodology:*** Teaching of Languages, Environmental Studies and Mathematics, Nature and Meaning of various School Subjects, Aims and Objectives of Languages, Environmental Studies and Mathematics, Curriculum, Planning of Teaching, Teaching Methods, Co-relation of School Subjects, Text Books, Museums, Laboratories, Libraries, Teacher, Creativity in Teaching, Problems of Classrooms, Utilisation of Community Resources, Dealing with Special Children Evaluation.

6. ***Practical Work:*** Preparation of Lesson Plans, Simulated Teaching, Improvisation of Teaching Aids, Participation in Community Development Activities, Fields Visits, Creative Activities.

7. ***Examinations:*** Candidates will be examined both by course faculty out side teacher educators, i.e., internal and external evaluation.

8. ***Faculty:*** Teaching faculty members as guest lecturers will be drawn from the local Colleges of Education and District Institutes of Education and Training. Faculty from other educational institutions and schools may also be utilised.

9. ***Duration of the Course:*** 30 days with 210 credit hours.

10. ***Eligibility:*** +2, U.G. and P.G. holders.

Time-Table for Each Session of Training

Classes will run between 8.00 a.m and 4.45 p.m. Number of classes per each day will be 7. No holidays will be there during the programme.

Period	Time	Subject
1.	8.00—9.00 a.m.	Teacher and Education
2.	9.00—10.00 a.m.	Educational Psychology
3.	10.15—11.15 a.m.	Perspectives of Education
4.	11.15—12.15 Noon	Practical Work
5.	1.30—2.30 p.m.	Teaching Methodology
6.	2.30—3.30 p.m.	Educational Technology
7.	3.45—4.45 p.m.	Practical Work

According to the convenience of the candidates and availability of faculty members, necessary adjustments may be made in the time-table, but the work would be the same without any modification.

CONCLUSION

This short-term programme will serve very effectively the needs in the classrooms of untrained teachers and teacher aspirants and will also help in the promotion of educational development and nation building.

Digumarti Bhaskara Rao
R.V.R. College of Education
Guntur—522 006

14

Innovations and New Experiences in the Field of Teacher Education

Introduction

The report of the International Commission on Education for the Twenty-first Century, published in 1996, observed that: 'The importance of the role of the teacher as an agent of change, promoting understanding and tolerance, has never been more obvious than today. It is likely to become even more critical in the twenty-first century'.

In that same year, the forty-fifth session of the International Conference on Education (ICE) was held in Geneva devoted to 'Strengthening the role of the teacher in a changing world. The discussions during the Conference brought to light the major changes that are taking place in our societies, as illustrated by, among other things, the forceful arrival on the scene everywhere of the new information technologies; the globalization of the economy and the evolution that all professions are experiencing. These events have led to a profound reorganisation of education systems and, in this context, to a redefinition of the role of the teacher, both as the agent of change and the driving force of change. Themes concerning the quality of education and the quality of teachers were also the focus of discussions during the Education Commission of the twenty-ninth session of the General Conference of UNESCO, which took place during the months of October and November 1997. Delegates emphasized the polyvalent nature of the teacher's role which should allow them to teach both in the formal and the non-formal domains.

In the context of follow-up to the forty-fifth session of the ICE and of the Report of the International Commission on Education for the Twenty-first Century, the IBE is continuing to publish information about experiments and innovatory experiences, as well as statistics concerning teachers. These have been assembled mainly from the national reports on the development of education and the replies of Member States to the pre-conference survey carried out by the IBE on the theme of teachers.

TEACHER RECRUITMENT

Recommendation no. 1 of the forty-firth session of the International Conference on Education was concerned with attracting the most competent young people to the teaching profession.

Egypt

"Special Procedures for Encouraging Admission to the Faculties of Education"

The State embarked upon steps to encourage outstanding students to enrol themselves in faculties of education as a way of enhancing the quality of education, particularly through granting them financial incentives. To achieve this goal, the Supreme Council for the Universities (SCU) agreed on granting students achieving 70% of the total points possible 80 Egyptian pounds to be continued in the subsequent years of training provided that they obtained a general grading of 'good'. Moreover, the top thirty students of the scientific division and the top ten students of the literary division are granted 120 Egyptian pounds a year beyond the continuation of their annual remuneration, provided that they obtain a grade 'very good', and another remuneration of 120 Egyptian pounds in the event that he/

she obtains the grade 'excellent' during the promotion examination diploma. Such rules are applied impartially to male or female students who obtained their diploma at a teachers' institute attached to faculties of education.

Ethiopia

"Recruitment into the Teaching Profession": In order to attract the ablest young people into the teaching profession, every year professional awareness orientation programmes are conducted at the regional level. To increase the participation of women and students from disadvantaged regions in the teaching profession, the admission requirements are relaxed, a certain percentage of the quota is reserved for them, and special tutorial classes are given so that they are able to reach the same level as the other trainees.

Israel

"Criteria for Acceptance of Students": The criteria for acceptance of candidates for teaching positions include the countrywide qualifying 'threshold' examination. It serves as a prerequisite for acceptance to any institution in the system. An efficient battery of tests for the selection of candidates, one that would include cognitive and personality indices, still requires research. An alternative instrument for the selection of candidates, now being prepared and tested, includes-in addition to the cognitive aspect-a personality evaluation. It also includes a questionnaire inquiring about the candidate's predisposition for the teaching profession.

Canada

"Different Factors Taken into Consideration in Selecting Candidates": The majority of university faculties of education base their decisions on a combination of educational and personal factors, such as child empathy, statements by the candidate and references. When universities resort to interviews, it is in order to evaluate factors such as motivation, communication skills, the ability for rapid and effective action, the degree of interpersonal skills, creativity, compassion, determination, enthusiasm, maturity and leadership potential. The University of Ottawa has incorporated into its evaluation process an assessment of candidates' statements by three classroom teachers. Some universities are looking for candidates for specific disciplines. This is the case, for example, of Trent University in Peterborough (Ontario), which gives preference to candidatures with experience of special needs education or of multicultural education, as well as to women who intend to teach science.

Thailand

"Khuru Thayat Project to Attract Qualified Young People to Teaching": There are two courses under this Project: a one-year post-graduate course; and a five-year undergraduate course. Under the one-year course, university graduates from various faculties who have good academic and behavioural records and a positive attitude towards the teaching profession, will undergo intensive post-graduate training. The secondary school graduates admitted to the undergraduate course must have good academic records, good conduct, and positive attitudes towards the teaching profession. Throughout the five years, the students will have to reside in the college dormitory. Being boarders, the students can train together and join in various activities that contribute towards being a professional teacher. To stay in the course, the students must obtain a minimum of 2.75 grade point average each year and are required to attend an annual intensive summer course. Each student is given a scholarship. Most graduates under the Project are appointed to teach in their hometown.

Egypt

"Recruitment of Unemployed University Graduates to Teach in Literacy Classes": In collaboration with the social fund for development, a project was launched in 1992/93 to enrol unemployed university graduates to teach in classrooms for eradicating illiteracy. Based on the success of the project, its scope was widened to cover twenty districts in 1994/95. Approximately 27,000 university graduates were employed to eradicate illiteracy among 540,000 persons.

PRE-SERVICE TRAINING

Recommendation no. 2 of the forty-fifth session of the International Conference on Education was concerned with aligning pre-service training with the needs of an innovatory professional practice.

United Arab Emirates

"Affiliated Tutorial External Studies to Qualify Teachers for the Primary Stage": After the completion of their diploma courses, graduate completing pre-service teacher training are accommodated into university programmes to complete their educational qualification in specializations compatible with their original choices. This programme has directed young men to the profession of teaching and has provided the educational process with enormous numbers of teachers. Experience shows that there is a remarkable growth in the degree of performance at the basic stage from teachers who have completed their university studies.

Finland

"Teacher Education Units": Beyond faculties of education, the comprehensive school and upper secondary school-teachers are trained also at teacher-education units at universities. Each teacher-education unit has a teacher-training school or schools for practice and research. These training schools comprise a lower and upper stage of comprehensive school and an upper secondary school, and in some cases also pre-school.

Finland

"Class Teacher Education": Class teacher education is an interdisciplinary master's degree which requires a total of 160 credits. In addition to educational studies, it includes basic studies in several subjects, more advanced studies in one or two subjects and practice as follows: *(a)* general studies: 15 credits minimum; *(b)* pedagogic: 75 credits; *(c)* basic studies in several subjects: 35 credits; *(d)* specialized studies: 30–35 credits; *(e)* optional courses.

Belize

"Three-Year Certificate Programme with School Experience": The programme is aimed at temporary teachers who are not sufficiently qualified. The new programme can be pursued through two modes: *(a)* one-year full-time studies at the college (Level 1), followed by one to two years of experience in the field, and returning to the college for one additional year of full-time studies at Level 2; *(b)* two-and-a-half years in the extramural programme (Level 1), utilizing distance learning materials, followed by one year of full-time studies at the college to obtain Level 2. Teachers receive a salary increase after successfully completing Level 1 and another after successfully, completing Level 2.

Morocco

"New Procedures in the Content of Pre-Service Training": In an attempt to raise professional standards and to establish a standard form of training, teacher preparation is undergoing a fundamental questioning of its professional requirements in order to establish its training needs. Another matter being examined is the introduction of modular training in order to avoid problems arising from isolation and to satisfy the needs of overall training. Thus, stress is being placed on skills rather than on content. The role of educational research is perceived more and more as a core element of training. Concerning the introduction of new educational technologies, emphasis is being placed on the educational benefits to be derived from these technologies (computers and audio-visual aids). Beyond disciplinary, teaching and educational matters, training centres are organising activities designed to make future teachers aware of environmental and intercultural problems, as well as the ethical and moral aspects of the teaching profession.

Czech Republic

"New Contents of Teacher Training": The current conception of teacher training envisages the preparation of future teachers in the following basic components: study of the chosen specilization;

methodological preparation; teaching and psychological preparation. Added to these three components of general education which provides the future teachers with a broad cultural foundation, including knowledge of foreign languages. This component contributes to the teacher becoming a cultural authority whose function is to influence the general cultural background and moral and ethical character of the pupils/students. The newly drafted educational 'profile' of the teachers describes individual components as 'modules'. The proportion of final training represented by each individual module within the complex system is precisely defined. At the same time, the draft defines precisely the requirements to be achieved for the adequate performance of the teaching profession. The draft also reflects the effort required to create a more organic connection between educational and psychological theory and teaching practice. It is especially in the lower classes of schools that the effort to emphasize the practice-oriented training in social communication and methodological skills, and in diagnozing the personalities of the pupils/students, appears to be extremely important. Teaching practice focuses on monitoring the child and on co-operating with the child in the positive communicative environment of the classroom and in the whole school. Self-reflection on the part of the student-teachers is another important element of the teaching practice.

France

"The Way Teacher Training is Conceived in University Institutes of Teacher Training": The setting up of university institutes of teacher training (IUFM) was an opportunity to re-focus a part of training on the curriculum and to define it, at least for the primary level, in relation to a range of skills by linking it to both educational content and teaching skills. For future primary schools teachers, the objective is to 'universalize' training; for the secondary level, it is to strengthen professional preparation. The philosophy of the teacher training provided by the IUFM is based on an intensive alignment of theoretical work taking place in the IUFM and practical class work. The IUFMs, therefore, depend upon a network of primary and secondary schools and colleges, and where this important aspect of training takes place. On this point, the role of mobile teacher trainers in schools is vital. Each teacher-training institute establishes its training scheme according to a national chart of disciplines, timetables, etc., which is adapted to its own needs. In other words it is adapted to the people to be trained and to the various types of classes and schools where beginning teachers will work (secondary schools, pre-university, special assignments, multiple class schools in rural areas, etc.)

IN-SERVICE TRAINING

Recommendation no. 3 of the forty-fifth session of the International Conference on Education was concerned with in-service teacher training, which was to be conceived as a right, but also a duty for the entire teaching professional.

Australia

"Competency Based Training (CBT)": 'CBT is Action' is a national scheme which uses action learning to support the professional development of people committed to the implementation of the national training reform agenda in Australia. It is aimed at teachers, trainers, managers and associated staff. The scheme brings together a team of people in a specific work-place who are challenged with implementing a particular aspect of CBT. The team works on the project for an agreed amount of time. Members acquire the necessary knowledge and skills as the project develops. This is done through a combination of external training activities (literature, workshops, consultants, industrial visits, etc.) initiated by the team itself and by encouraging creative insight. Improved understanding of CBT challenges the participants to review and reflect on what they are learning, and where necessary, to reinterpret any preconceived ideas they may have had. The introduction of CBT has required any preconceived ideas they may have had. The introduction of CBT has required significant changes in the design and delivery of training programmes and courses, because the focus is placed primarily on outcomes, i.e. on work-place competencies the participant can actually demonstrate as a result of the teaching/learning process.

Cồte d'ivoire

The Training of Educational Advisers: In order to raise the intellectual level of educational advisers, sixty regional advisers and responsible for the training of sectoral educational advisers. The regional advisers are instructors from educational training centres (pre-service teacher training) with a higher level of training than the former advisers, who were merely former teachers. One trained, the sectoral advisers must pass on to the teachers for whom they are responsible the lessons learned in their respective fields.

Switzerland

"The Training of Trainers": The present tendency for all teacher training to take place at the university level has highlighted gaps that exist in scientific disciplines. In response to this need, the University of Bern provided to subject-teaching instructors a course in the teaching of each discipline—a course that leads to a diploma.

There also exists in French-speaking Switzerland an official course for subject-teaching instructors. These efforts by the authorities can be illustrated by an example from the canton of Vaud: 'The creation of the post of qualified teacher trainer'; the training specifically required to work in teacher training in French-speaking Switzerland; the participation of teacher trainers in cantonal commissions on various disciplines in order to ensure a direct link between the evolution of disciplines and the training of young teachers; follow-up with the appropriate faculties (University of Lausanne) with a view to equating the university studies of future teachers with the actual needs of teaching.

Jordan

"Training Programme to Meet Challenges in the Field of Education for Democracy, Peace, Conflict Resolution and Human Rights": The programme objectives include: *(a)* preparing training modules dealing with issues of international understanding, democracy, justice, peace, human rights, and cultural pluralism; *(b)* equipping teachers with skills to deal with these issues intelligently;

(c) exchanging experiences with other countries on methods used to deal with these issues; and *(d)* transferring the training outcomes into the classrooms. The initial stage of the programme aims at training a pivotal team of five persons to lead this project; training a twenty-six-person team for regional training in the north, middle and south regions; and training seventy-five teachers during a trial stage to assess the effectiveness of the training activities and the trainers. The training contents include the following: *(a)* values and attitudes which deal with the issues and challenges revealed in the religious doctrines and social habits of the Arabic and Islamic nations; (b) values are attitudes which deal with the issues and challenges revealed in the religious doctrines of the Jaws and Christians. Training methods consist of discussions, argumentation, role playing, showing films, wall charts and brochures, and designing activities to be included in the teacher's guides.

Kenya

"In-Service Course Programme for Primary Teachers": The in-service programmes is an innovative approach for training teachers. Whereas the traditional primary teacher training mode lasts two years, the in-service course in staggered over three years but covers the same curriculum content as pre-service training. The course is divided into four components: correspondence, residential, radio and teaching assessment. The correspondence component covers 75% and resident component 25% of the course syllabus. The radio component supplements whatever is covered by the correspondence and residential components. In the teaching assessment component, school inspectors visit trainee teachers in their respective schools and assess them as they work in the classroom. Every trainee teacher is assessed at least nine times during the three years of the course.

Canada

"The Ontario Educational Network": The purpose of this project is to facilitate communication and access to resources for all classroom teachers with a view to reforming the curriculum: *(a)* an electronic network linking computers allows teachers to discuss different aspects of the reform and the changes being introduced; *(b)* a team of change agents assists teachers in the planning of change; *(c)* a communication programme enables teachers to share their experiences among themselves. This service is provided free of charge. School councils use the network to establish their plans; teachers unions use it to send material connected with the programme leading to the qualification of inspector as well as for a large number of conferences. It is hoped to extend the system to the student population. At present, a way is being sought to use the network to make in-service training programmes available.

France

"Training School Inspectors and Managers": In 1995, the National Training Centre for Inspectors and Managers became the Higher School for Staff Attached to the Ministry of National Education (Ecole supérieure des personnels d'encadrement du ministère de l'éducation nationale—ESPEMEN). The training scheme was prepared according to three major lines: *(a)* The *principle of alternation:* the training period foresees part of the time spent studying and part of the time working in the field. By insisting on the unified nature of the training, it is evident that the time spent in the field is an integral part of the training, and not simply a posting. For each specilization, a list of professional situations has been prepared. These situations, requiring training, represent in themselves a way of analysing the professional problems each requiring further intervention by the training school and the field units. *(b) The principle of individuality:* the type of participant, adults who have already acquired vocational skills, as well as the nature of the training, vocational conversion, suggest that the training paths should be individualized. This breaking down of the training course is based on the candidate's previous experiences. *(c) Coherence:* overall coherence of the training programme is guaranteed by the way in which the content is structured and by the alternation over time between study and field work. The training scheme has been guided by the desire to create the conditions for an understanding to come to the fore about the common responsibility for training for the various functions through: common content designed to acquire wide-ranging skills (processing the necessary information for the development of the education system, checking that actions and practices are relevant, organising the way in which a service or unit functions, mobilizing the participants, establishing relations with partners, training human resources, evaluating changing situations, directing a fluctuating sub-system, assuming the role of representative of an institution); a deeper understanding of common content, the way different trades operate, the specific content of each particular trade listed in a directory, knowledge of teaching skills, law and administration, directing and managing human resources.

Uganda

"Primary Education and Teacher Development Project (PETDP), Teacher Development and Management System (TDMS) Component": Following the White Paper on Education issued in 1992, the Government decided to establish a Teacher Development and Management System (TDMS) in ten of the thirty-eight districts of Uganda. The project has the following objectives, among others: to up-grade teacher training facilities; to improve teacher support infrastructure; to ensure more effective use of teacher training resources; to improve quality and effectiveness of primary teachers' colleges (PTCs) graduates; to decrease the number of untrained teachers; to up-grade the skills and effectiveness of practising teachers. TDMS consists of a system of reformed or 'core' PTCs, each of which is linked to about twenty-five 'co-ordinating centres' (CC), each of which, in turn, in turn, is linked to a surrounding network of about ten 'outreach schools' (OS). The core PTCs which join the TDMS network have four tasks: *(a)* pre-service training of new teachers; *(b)* in-service up-grading of practising teachers through vacation courses and distance education; *(c)* on-going in-service training to bring new methods, texts and learning materials to teachers in the schools; and *(d)* management training and support for teachers and head teachers. There are also a large number of tutors to deliver TDMS teacher/community/pupil component services. An on-campus faculty handles all the courses that are conducted at the PTC, and an off-campus faculty is responsible for the academic and professional aspects at CCs and OSs. There is one tutor permanently based at each of the CCs who is assisted by visiting PTC tutors, inspectors of schools and education officers. One of the major roles of the resident tutors at a CC, is to maintain a link with the core PTC, the CC and OSs. OS tutors, known as personal tutors, are expected to keep the resident CC tutor well informed about the performance of the student-teachers under their care. This programme is characterized by flexibility in terms of course component, modes of learning, learner control and choice regarding the content time, place and method of learning and learner-support systems.

ASSISTANCE TO BEGINNING TEACHERS

'Special attention should be paid to teachers at the beginning of their career, since the initial positions that they will hold and the tasks they will perform will have a decisive effect on the remainder of their training and career' (Extract from Recommendation no. 3 of the forty-fifth session of the International Conference on Education.)

Australia

"Teacher Induction": Teacher induction is a direct responsibility of education systems that employ a variety of approaches. The purpose of these schemes is to provide support and guidance for the beginning teacher and facilitate a smooth transition into the teaching profession. Examples of induction include; distribution of an induction kit supported by mentoring programmes; a formal induction programme; and probation or appraisal period involving assessment and evaluation.

Australia

"National Competency Standards for Beginning Teachers": The development of national competency standards for teachers arose from the broad context of award restructuring and from moves towards mutual recognition of qualifications. In the teaching profession, these broad initiatives are aimed at removing barriers and impediments to improving the quality of teaching, and hence, learning outcomes for Australia's students. A 'Competency Framework for Beginning Teachers' has been developed. The framework articulates the key and essential areas of competence for teaching, elements for each area of competence and indicators of effective practice for each element. It is supported by a set of brief case studies illustrating the competencies.

Czech Republic

"Support for Beginning Teachers": Each beginning teacher must have at least ten weeks of teaching practice at a school or at another educational institution. During his/her first year in service the young teacher is assisted by an experienced mentor who helps him or her to overcome the initial difficulties. The mentor's assistance comprises a variety of activities, such as mutual observations of classes, analyses of the teaching process, discussions about the methods and contents of the classes, introduction to the social and professional life of the staff, consultations with pupils/students and with parents.

Germany

"Preparatory Service for Young Graduates": Young graduates have a practical introduction in the form of the preparatory service, constituting the second stage of student-teachers' training, which can last up to two years. Thanks to this preparatory service, students can combine the knowledge and skills they have acquired during their academic university studies with practical and pedagogical knowledge, and skills and experience necessary to do their job. In terms of didactic training, the primary task of this preparatory phase is to give prospective teachers the skills they will require in their complex role as teachers, counsellors and educators, thus enabling them to perform their duties in line with their individual capabilities. Young graduates gain these skills by; sitting in on, and observing, lessons; teaching lessons in schools involved in teacher training—either under the guidance of a tutor or on their own—as well as attending further

courses in teaching methods at training centres where the experiences students have gained in the classroom can be worked on and analysed in greater depth.

Source: *Educational Innovation and Information* (published by International Bureau of Education—UNESCO, Geneva), Number 93, pp: 2—7.

Courtesy: International Bureau of Education, Geneva, Switzerland.

15

Strengthening the Role of Teachers in a Changing World

The forty-fifth session of the International Conference on Education (ICE) took place between 30 September and 5 October 1996; it was devoted to a discussion of 'Straightening of the role of teachers in a changing world'. This theme was selected not only because of the concern brought about by the present situation, but even more so due to apprehension concerning the future. The teachers of the next century are those young people who today are deciding to join the teaching profession. It is therefore today that decisions about their recruitment, training, professional support and career prospects must be defined.

The Conference has been prepared following a series of regional meetings and these regional meetings have enabled to appreciate the wide diversity of existing situations. However, despite the diversity of those situations, a common opinion emerged from all of these discussions: educational reforms intended to confront the challenges of the future must reach the educational establishment and the classroom. Awareness of this fact means that the teachers play the key role in the future process of transforming education.

The experience of recent decades has confirmed that it is not possible to continue reforming education systems without taking the teachers into consideration; but, on the contrary, it was also confirmed that we cannot ask teachers to change without education itself changing. The success of education policies depends to a great extent on the integrated nature of their training.

On this point, the regional discussions have enabled at least four fundamental aspects to be identified:

1. The professionalization of teaching activity is the best long term strategy to improve the outcomes of education and, at the same time, the working conditions of teachers.
2. Pre-service and in-service training should be profoundly modified so as to enable teachers to gain mastery of the whole range of educational strategies adapted to the wide diversity of learning situations with which they will be confronted in carrying out their duties. This diversity and wide-range of situations can only be managed by teachers working as a team, and not as isolated individuals.
3. Teachers must learn to use the new information technologies. This means that the new technologies must no longer be perceived either as a threat or as a panacea able to overcome all problems; this matter must be openly discussed, without prejudice or preconceptions, for a number of these misconceptions are based on a misunderstanding of reality.
4. Finally, all the discussions which took place during the preparation of the ICE indicate that more than more will be expected of future teachers, whether it be a question of ethical training, training for tolerance, or the ability to manage uncertainty, creativity, solidarity or participation. Teachers will therefore be appreciated not only for their knowledge and purely technical skills, but also for their personal qualities. To be more exact, this means that the personal qualities of the teacher will be increasingly considered as indispensable technical requirement for carrying out the profession.

I. SUMMARY OF REGIONAL PREPARATORY MEETINGS FOR THE ICE

Five preparatory meetings were held in collaboration with UNESCO's Regional Offices and, in the European case, with the Polish Ministry of National Education, the Polish National Commission for (UNESCO) and the Council of Europe.

These meetings carried out an analysis of the situation concerning teachers in their respective regions and put forward proposals for the ICE. More than 200 representatives of governments, experts invited in a personal capacity as well as representatives of various IGOs and NGOs were involved in this process of consultation prior to the ICE.

The regional meetings agreed on the main trends and concerns regarding teachers. These involved three aspects:

- The need for further professionalization of the teaching vocation, as well as for more commitment and responsibility on the part of teachers;
- A deterioration in the social standing of teachers;
- A deterioration in working conditions, including teachers' salaries in real terms and sometimes in terms of the actual amount.

Participants observed that teacher morale had gone down almost everywhere, standards have dropped and commitment is slowly being eroded away.

The African Region

UNESCO Office, Dakar, Senegal, 11—13 March 1996

The participants at this meeting considered that it was a matter of priority of launch educational reforms that could anticipate the future needs of society in the twenty-first century in a world strongly dominated by technology.

Teachers in Africa are not sufficiently well prepared to meet the reality which confronts them in schools: over-populated classes, curricula that undergo constant changes as a result of the demands of society in constant evolution, and the new requirements of an introduction to science and technology. The emergency programmes that are frequently put forward to resolve these problems are often not appropriate, since they are frequently out of step with reality. The participants agreed that questions concerning the training and well-being of teachers should be dealt with in conformity with established policies and that the problems facing teachers should not be tackled in a haphazard way.

Participants at the meeting were convinced that candidates entering teacher-training programmes should be selected for their moral and intellectual suitability, and should have successfully completed their secondary studies.

The question of the length of training programmes—either part-time or full-time—should be decided according to the established objectives for the acquisition of the required knowledge and skills. Participants stressed the need for trainee teachers to acquire sufficient educational skills through practical experience carried out in the classroom.

During their training, teachers should also be introduced to research methods in science and technology, as well as to new teaching methods and the use of computers. Training programmes should give teachers an opportunity to choose their specialization: computer-assisted teaching, evaluation methods, the ability to manage school libraries, sports programmes, and educational broadcasts.

Confronted with the information explosion, it is difficult for teachers by themselves to master the transmission of knowledge and to keep up to date with progress. The participants therefore considered it necessary to redefine the role of the teacher given the new methods of acquiring and transferring information. Teachers should be able to give their pupils skills in the fields of research and lifelong self-education.

The participants expressed their concern with the working conditions of African Teachers. They suported UNESCO's position which foresaw that in no case should structural adjustment measures have a negative effect on education systems and the teaching staff.

Participants also expresed their concern that even 'the oldest technologies' were not available in schools. Computerized equipment has now become a priority but, at the same time, the production of simple teaching materials by the teachers themselves should be encouraged. The usefulness of distance education technique was also recognized.

It was proposed that each Member State should set up a council of teachers at the national level to follow up and deal with their problems. The regional meting stressed the importance of the joint Recommendation on the status of teachers through which the ILO and UNESCO put forward conditions for the recruitment, training, employment, service and well being of teachers.

As far as teachers' salaries were concerned, the meeting considered that the deplorable economic state of African governments could not be used as an excuse to overlook the arrears in teachers' salaries and other inhuman actions.

In the opinion of the participants, governments and society do not seem to appreciate the full importance of teachers. It was proposed to organise activities and awareness—raising, campaigns for the general public. The celebration of International Teachers' Day on 5 October could present the ideal opportunity.

Given that many teachers work in rural communities, it was suggested that they should be offered special concessions in recognition of the difficulties facing them.

The administration should not be left to manage the education system on its own, since this leads to a certain frustration among teachers. The meeting believed that teachers should be involved in educational decision-making at all levels.

It was suggested that centres for promoting co-operation and collaboration amongst teachers should be created.

Asia and Pacific Region

Bangkok, Thailand, 18—19 April, 1996

This regional meeting pointed out that any meaningful enhancement of the role of teachers in a changing world involves two necessary pre-conditions: *(a)* the recognition of a changing world and the identification of present and likely future change agents; and *(b)* the re-engineering of education at least in terms of the curriculum, pedagogy, teacher education (including the recruitment of teachers), partnerships in education and the organisational context of teaching.

Governments should take the lead in the determination of a new profile for teachers in terms of teaching competencies, management skills, professional duties and responsibilities, personal attributes and quality control.

With the declared intention of enhancing the status of teachers, governments should commission working parties, representative of all those concerned by education: *(a)* to identify factors determining the status of teachers ('status' to be viewed broadly in personal, professional and social terms); *(b)* to formulate proposals to enhance the status of teachers; *(c)* to set an order of priorities and to estimate the cost of the proposals; and *(d)* to propose a programme for implementation of the proposals.

Governments should monitor teacher education programmes with a view to:

(a) targeting teachers as prime candidates for lifelong education—from recruitment to retirement;

(b) ensuring that teachers are provided with adequate life-long education to meet the demands placed on them for teaching in a changing society;

(c) ensuring that teacher education providers and programmes fully accorded with the new paradigms for the new profiling

of teachers, the enhancement of their status and other critical matters, especially in terms of lifelong (in-service) education.

Given the benefits and burdens that new information technologies bring to the role and functions of teachers. It is in the interest of governments—as and when new information technologies become available: *(a)* to ensure that teachers become computer literate; *(b)* to provide teachers with the most user-friendly technological resources (and appropriate support services); and *(c)* to assess the efficiency pedagogically and economically) of technology as a means for delivering educational services.

As custodians of educations as a public good, the policy and resourcing of education rest ultimately with the governments, as does the direction of educational change in an evolving world. But the management of that change should involve teachers committed to educational change. Equally, all those with an interest in the evolution of education should be involv~d in partnership as participative change agents.

Arab States

University of Al-Ain,
United Arab Emirates, 8—10 April 1996

The regional meeting pointed out that, despite the progress achieved by Arab States in the Field of universalization of education, the eradication of illiteracy and advances in the quality of education, Arab teachers still do not enjoy an appropriate socio-economic status likely to attract qualified people to the teaching profession.

The most serious constraint facing the upgrading of educational quality in the Arab States in the existing gap between the actual requirements for carrying out teaching and those of professionalization.

Participants also stressed the need for updating legislation so as to render laws more appropriate to the multiple roles of teachers, and to grant them adequate autonomy making it easier for them to fulfil their new roles.

The participants stressed the need for the professionalization of teaching. They also emphasized the importance of defining teaching competencies. This means that joining the teaching profession should be subject to passing specially designed tests, at the same time as developing criteria which would ensure selection of talented people with appropriate qualification for the teaching profession, and adopting a system for incentives. The necessary measures should also be taken to involve teachers in planning and developing educational progammes.

The meeting also highlighted several aspects in favour of teachers' pre-service and in-service training programmes, taking into consideration that such programmes should be based on clearly defined teaching skills, and should maintain a balance among academic, educational and professional elements. Such training should include current issues, such as population, environmental and health education, as well as international co-operation, and concentrate on training teachers to employ methods likely to develop the intellectual and emotional potential of their students. Teachers should also be trained to deal with the varied needs, abilities and aptitudes of students. Participants emphasized that these programmes should be future-oriented and stressed the need for improving the provision of model educational technologies, as well as continuous teacher training on the effective use of these technologies.

The meeting called upon mass media institutions to design and develop programmes that enhance the teacher's role and social status, and improve his/her image as an agent of social change;

It also emphasized the importance of the UNESCO/ILO Recommendation concerning the Status of Teachers (1966).

European Region

Warsaw, Poland, 25—26 April 1996

The meeting mentioned the significant changes that are typical of societies at this end of century, and which affect education systems, notably:

- A more profound search for answers in questions concerning daily life as well as a greater demand for democratic participation;
- Greater heterogeneity in the school population due, among other thing, to the emergence of societies that are increasingly multi or pluricultural; there was acceptance of the important role that the school can play as an integrating factors;
- An increasing demand for a more lengthy training process;
- The information explosion and its spread thanks to new technologies;
- A sometimes troubled relationship between education and the economy; an increase in unemployment among young people;
- A widespread crisis in public finances;
- A risk that reference points will weaken or disappear in as much as values or standards are concerned which may, among other things, fuel feelings of intolerance and violence;
- A widespread movement towards decentralization;
- A certain erosion of confidence in education systems and teachers in general.

The meeting put forward the key points of a 'reply which education systems, and particularly teachers, could provide by stressing the following.

- The need for adaptation, for reform and sometimes, even a total 'recasting' of education systems;
- A redefinition of objectives as well as a reasonable re-focusing on what is expected of the school and teaching;
- Widespread agreement in order to better confront resistance to change and/or the pressures of particular lobbies;

- The emergence of a new conception of the school as a learning centre and a collective enterprise to which each must contribute with his/her own skills;
- The limits to which the economic principles of free enterprise can be applied to the education system;
- The need for public authorities to take full responsibility for their role in promoting equality of opportunity, access to education, social cohesion and the advancement of democratic values;
- The need to make bridges with the economy;
- The interest in promoting educational research, comparative studies and action research directly linked with the school's reality;
- The new stress to be placed on the processes and methodologies of school management, autonomy of the educational team and collaboration among all the different actors;
- The redefinition of roles, profiles, and the training of teachers;
- The necessity for the school and the teachers to place values at the very centre of their concerns and to develop among the learners an attitude of openness encouraging ideas of peace, tolerance and respect for human dignity;
- Strengthening exchanges and existing networks at the international and regional levels, and promoting solidarity among teachers;
- The professionalization of the teaching vocation;
- The opening up of the school and teachers to the outside world;
- Taking the internationalization of relations and the increasing mobility of people into account during training which will require the introduction of a European—and global—dimension at school;

- Training teachers in inter-cultural pedagogy;
- Training for teamwork, autonomy and solidarity;
- The evaluation of teachers and of institutions.

The meeting also stressed the importance of partnership as a participative and co-operative approach. Since partnership is one way of opening it could involve the level of the school as well as the local, regional and national dimensions.

The enormous potential represented by new information and communication technologies to improve education was recognized. From this it follows that education systems must incorporate and learn to master them in order to avoid any subservience to technology, culture or the economy, as well as any risk of the school being isolated to the fringes compared with other sectors. The introduction of new technologies, does not however, diminish the essential role of the teacher which consists of, on the one hand, arranging information so that it becomes knowledge, the ability to make choices and to develop a critical attitude and, on the other, the transmission of culture.

On the subject of the training of trainers, the consultation proposed that:

- They are themselves trained to cope with change;
- They themselves participate in lifelong training in the schools;
- They play a significant role with young teachers.

Latin America and the Caribbean

Kingston, Jamaica, 13-17 May 1996. Organised in the context of the seventh Regional Conference of Ministers of Education (MINEDLAC VII).

Matters concerning the ICE were specifically dealt with during a round-table on "The teaching profession and the development of education in Latin America and the Caribbean; strengthening the role of teachers in a changing world'.

The participants expressed the opinion that necessary change must be focused on two areas; the political and administrative structure of education; and the teachers themselves. They stressed the need of each educator to develop as a citizen, a professional and an individual. To this end, the following proposals were made:

- to review the profile of the teacher before and after training;
- certification as a prerequisite for all teaching activity;
- incentive programmes based on performance;
- accreditation for faculties of education based on the highest international standards;
- and guidance for the teacher in creating a new organisational climate.

Five area were highlighted in teacher training; self-reliance; intellectual autonomy; social and emotional independence; skill in handling technology; and the development of artistic judgement.

One of the participants spoke of the fallacy of claiming that teachers could be competitive and competent when they were left out of the modernization process and when problems persisted regarding pay and minimal resources in schools.

A wide-ranging debate took place focusing on; the need to seek innovative and unconventional solutions to complex problems; a re-evaluation of teacher-training institutions, an overhaul of the teaching profession, with acknowledgment of its autonomy; a review of the institutional factors preventing teachers from renewing their skills and assuming fresh challenges; the important role of the head teacher and the staff; and the need to identify priority in action plans. Despite the complexity of the problem, emphasis was placed on the need to continue to make progress by: recognizing all factors; laying down priorities and sequences of operations; and encouraging creativity in order to take full advantage of the educational resources of society.

The meeting particularly insisted on encouraging the development of a positive social image of the teaching career and designing long-term training plans for in-service teachers so as to professionalize and broaden the outlook for education.

II. DRAFT RECOMMENDATIONS OF THE 45TH SESSION OF THE INTERNATIONAL CONFERENCE ON EDUCATION

Foreword

1. Thirty years after the adoption by UNESCO and ILO of the Recommendation concerning the Status of Teachers (1996) and 21 years after the thirty-fifth session of the International Conference on Education, which also dealt with the theme of teachers, the time has now come to examine once again the role, the functions and even the position of teachers and educators in schools and in society.

2. Indeed, globalization which is affecting the economy, culture and information, the internationalization of relations and the increasing mobility of individuals, a complete revolution in the communications media and the massive advent of computerization into daily life and into the world of work represent both a challenge and an opportunity to the education systems. At the same time, many societies and education systems are experiencing serious problems of social integration, among which should be mentioned inter-ethnic conflicts and violence, increasing unemployment—particularly among young people—a decline in moral values, the weakening of guidelines and changes in the role of family ties in the socialization of children. If all these challenges and problems are not overcome in the short term, there could be a risk or reinforcing feeling of uncertainty and pessimism that are particularly pernicious for future generations. Hopes on the part of societies, and especially the youth, for a more dignified, democratic and prosperous life and linked to education, which is considered to be the main instrument in the development of humanity.

3. While education is being transformed as a result of these changing, it is expected that teachers will educate, teach

guide and evaluate, and they will also demonstrate/their capacity to develop themselves, to participate in modernizing the school and to make it more practice and receptive to change. They should not only facilitate learning, but should also promote citizenship training and active integration into society, develop curiosity, critical thinking and creativity, initiative and self-determination. The role of the teacher will increasingly become that of a facilitator of learning within the group. Furthermore, confronted with the increasing role played by other information providers and socialization agents, it is expected that teachers will assume the role of moral and educational guide enabling learners to obtain their bearings in this mass of information and different values. It is through carrying out their functions as co-ordinator of educational activities provided by various partners—and directed towards common educational goals—that modern teachers will become effective agents of change in the community. Much is expected of education and teachers, too much perhaps, and not always for the right reasons, for, in the first place, it is society itself, clearly with the participation of the teacher, that is supposed to find a solution to its malfunctions.

4. It is not a question of putting forward a unique solution for all countries, but of establishing common guidelines. The variety of situations at the regional, national and local levels obviously implies that these guidelines should be adapted. There is, however, one essential condition; if this vast undertaking of educational renewal is to succeed, inevitably there has to be mutual confidence between teachers at all levels and administrators, all education staff and the public and private partners of education systems. In order to maintain such a climate there is a need to establish criteria which provide a clear definition of the competencies and roles of all those involved with respect to autonomy, responsibility and participation.

5. The implementation of the ILO/UNESCO Recommendation concerning the Status of Teachers were more difficult than foreseen. Two conclusions, however, can be drawn from

past experience and from the foundation for the present series of recommendations.

(i) political commitment and technical competence are both necessary to achieve the objectives set;

(ii) a systemic approach is absolutely indispensable. Experience has taught us that the teacher's role cannot be modified through isolated measures. The Recommendations of the forty-fifth session of the ICE should therefore be considered as an integrated whole.

6. Nevertheless, it should be noted that the living and working conditions of teachers and very often not commensurate with the important and significant task they perform. Three is thus a need to devote particular attention to this aspect and to spare no effort in making education a priority within development plans and in enhancing the status of teachers.

Recommendation No. 1

Recruitment of Teachers: Attracting the Most Competent Young People to Teaching

1. The recruitment of future teachers is of great concern to the educational authorities and specialists in many parts of the world. While national situations are highly diverse, in all the regional meetings of experts in preparation for the ICE, it was observed that the teaching profession is often not very attractive from the point of view of its social status and its development prospects.

2. The criteria for the recruitment of future teachers should not depend only on the knowledge base of applicants. Personal qualities, such as moral integrity, a sense of responsibility and of solidarity, motivation and a favourable attitude towards teamwork, and the ability to communicate are also necessary.

3. In this respect, the following measures are recommended:

(i) to undertake actions raising young people's awareness of the importance of the teaching profession and guiding

them towards it, through meetings with eminent teachers, public recognition of teachers, open days in schools and teacher education institutes, the reporting of innovatory experiences in schools and by teachers in the media, among others;

(ii) to offer incentives and scholarships to pupils and students with strong academic and extra-curricular records who wish to pursue a career in the teaching profession;

(iii) to promote gender equality by seeking a better balance of men and women in the teaching profession at all levels and in all academic disciplines;

(iv) to encourage qualified people coming from other professional fields to enter teaching, in order to overcome possible shortages of teaching staff, and to establish for this purpose appropriate recruiting and education arrangements;

(v) to develop and offer intellectually challenging programmes for teacher educators in order to prepare through them teachers of appropriate academic and professional qualifications and to attract the most competent young people to the teaching profession.

Recommendation No. 2

Pre-service Training: A Better Linkage between Pre-service Training and the Demands of an Innovatory Professional Activity.

1. In all parts of the world, it is possible to observe different levels of dissatisfaction about the pre-service training of teachers. In some cases, there is a wide gulf between inputs to teacher training and the demands that their professional activities should satisfy, particularly concerning: *(i)* their mastery of the discipline they are teaching; *(ii)* their grasp of the range of teaching strategies in the role that they are expected to play and in the diversity of teaching and learning situations; *(iii)* their keen interest in lifelong education; *(iv)* their ability to innovate and to work in a

team; and *(v)* their observance of professional ethics.

2. Pre-service training should be closely linked to in-service training. Building a unified teacher education and training system which views pre-service and in-service learning as a continuum is a concerned shared throughout the world.

3. In order to further improve pre-service training, the following measures are recommended:

(i) to associate mastery of the knowledge that the teacher should transmit with mastery of the teaching/learning methods appropriate to this knowledge. In this respect, it is necessary to strengthen the abilities which will enable future teachers to master a range of educational strategies to be used in the different situations and stages of the learning process, by integrating into their training methods of active learning that they will be expected to use during their professional career;

(ii) to strengthen the place of teaching practice during pre-service training, through methods employing observation, discussion and participation, both in regular situations, and during innovatory educational experiments and pedagogical research. Pre-service teacher training should grant priority to solving the major problems in each education system, such as training for teaching reading, writing and mathematics in both multilingual and monolingual contexts, training in the teaching of multi-grade classes and multi-cultural classes and training in modern approaches to learning assessment;

(iii) to develop basic skills among teachers for the performance of their indispensable role, which consists on the one hand in arranging information in such a way that it may become knowledge, in making choices and in developing critical faculties, and on the other hand in transmitting culture, forming personal and social relationships, being outgoing, favouring life together and promoting awareness of both differences and common values. In particulars, these skills involve;

In-service education: mastery of the subject, concepts, knowledge and pedagogical skills and integrating appropriate attitudes for the continuous updating of their professional qualifications, enabling them to adapt to the process of the evolution of knowledge and to the variety of educational problems to be resolved;

Teamwork: inculcating attitudes encouraging co-operation and dialogue with colleagues and all levels of educational staff, the essential conditions for collective professionalism guiding teaching activities;

Innovation and Experimentation: developing of a scientific outlook, basic training in methods of pedagogical research and active participation in the evaluation of experiments;

Respect for Others, Human Rights, Peace and Democracy: the personal conviction and the professional abilities to teach pupils to live together, to prevent and resolve conflicts, through dialogue and negotiation and to reject violence towards and intolerance of others;

Cultural Diversity: taking into account cultural diversity essential for mutual understanding in an inter-cultural/multi-cultural environment;

Respect for Nature: development for widespread awareness of the challenges to our environment and development of the professional ability to teach pupils to take individual and collective action aimed at protecting it;

(iv) to grant particular attention to the development among teachers of attitudes encouraging successful learning among their pupils, particularly those pupils from disadvantaged groups (physically, socio-economically and geographically) and from cultures different from the dominant one;

(v) to aim, both quantitatively and qualitatively, at training teachers able to satisfy the needs of different ethnic and cultural groups of those with special education needs and from remote regions, people living in extreme poverty or those affected by conflict.

Recommendation No. 3

In-Service Training: Both a Right and a Duty for All Educational Personnel

1. In a world undergoing rapid change, in-service training has become vital in carrying out all activities and professions. Thus, teachers are not only obliged to renew their skills continuously, but also to develop in their pupils the attitudes and skills required to create knowledge for themselves throughout their lives.

2. Regional analyses have shown that in-service training is the subject of considerable attention, both by the authorities and by teachers. Past experience and future challenges make it possible to predict the following main lines of action for in-service training policies in the future:

   (i) in-service training should be considered as both a right and a duty of educators. Care should be taken that a balanced approach to these two concepts is adopted, varying according to national situations and different periods. However, any in-service training policy should guarantee a minimum of training opportunities for all teachers;

   (ii) in-service training should be organised to a greater extent within educational establishment and through teamwork, with the active participation of the teachers themselves in defining the programme;

   (iii) special attention should be paid to teachers at the beginning of their career, since the initial positions that they will hold and the tasks they will perform will have a decisive effect on the remainder of their training and career. Tutorial and supervisory systems in the exercise of the profession should be introduced during the initial phases of their career;

   (iv) mechanisms which make it possible for pre-service training to benefit from the experience gained in in-

service training should be set up in order to give future teachers an opportunity to become acquainted with the problems encountered and the solutions adopted in a professional context;

(v) in-service training should also be developed through the medium of professional support services, which have been conceived as centres of assistance in solving problems, and to which all teachers should have access;

(vi) special priority should be given to the in-service training and education of those involved in the management, supervision and evaluation of teachers in order to enable them not only to play an administrative or supervisory role, but also to provide pedagogical guidance;

(vii) teacher trainers and teacher-training institutes should play an essential part in the process of strengthening the role of teachers and activity participate in their in-service training. In order for them to carry out this function, programmes should be developed and designed to make teacher trainers aware of the outcomes of pre-service training, and to provide permanent contact with researchers and scientists so as to ensure that their own training is up-to-date.

(viii) urgent action should be undertaken in areas where teachers are underqualified and untrained. This action should build upon the empirical skills already acquired by these teachers, as well as on their motivation and their knowledge of the local situation. Besides being a means of certification, this urgent action should strengthen the teachers' professional competence and upgrade their knowledge of current developments in pedagogy and subject matter, thus making in-service education a continuous process of educational renewal.

Recommendation No. 4

The Involvement of Teachers and Other Agents in the Process of Transforming Education: Autonomy and Responsibility

1. Transformation of education—no matter what the national characteristics are—is tending towards greater autonomy in educational decision making at the local and school levels, accompanied by a greater degree of responsibility concerning the outcomes.

2. To encourage the participation of teachers in the process of transforming education, the following measures could be implemented:

   (i) defining educational objectives and the directions of reforms through consultation, co-ordination and dialogue with teachers and their organisations in line with the provisions of the ILO/UNESCO Recommendation concerning the Status of Teachers and other agents in the transformation of education such as: the family, parents' association, businesses, employers, workers' organisations, the media, ethical and spiritual authorities and the scientific community. Such consultation and co-ordination should not be limited to the execution phase of projects or reforms, but should also concern their design, initiation, follow-up and evaluation;

   (ii) granting a sufficient degree of autonomy to educational establishments to enable them to make decisions concerning teaching and learning methods and the organisation of educational activities, and implementing systems for evaluating the outcomes, which have been conceived as factors for improving the quality of teaching and efficiency in the distribution of financial and human resources; similarly, strengthening the role of municipal and local authorities in advising schools so as to enable them to derive greater benefits from their autonomy;

(iii) proposing and implementing measures promoting educational innovation, for both individuals and establishments;

(iv) accompanying the process of strengthening the participation of teachers with appropriate measures for training, equipment and professional support services.

Recommendation No. 5

Teachers and Their Partners in the Educational Process: Education as a Responsibility for All

1. Ever since the Jomtien Conference, there has been general agreement that education is the responsibility of all and not of governments or of teachers alone. Partnership has become an essential element in the transformation of education in a world where knowledge and information are key factors in the economy and where respect for cultural diversity, gender equality and other human rights is vital for democratic stability. The forms of partnership are different depending upon cultural, political and administrative traditions, but regional discussions have allowed two main lines of action to be identified; opening up the school to the needs and requirements of the community; and enabling it to participate in community development activities. However, experiences of partnership have shown that this is not a simple or easy undertaking: partnerships succeed and fail: partners agree and disagree. The partnership route is not without its problems but provides a viable way forward compared with the isolationist alternative. Partnership should be conceived as a factor for improving the quality of learning; it should therefore not be perceived as an end in itself, as a way of removing responsibility from the State, from teachers and even from the community, but rather as an effective way of involving actors and exercising joint responsibilities.

2. Within the specific context of each national situation, the following measures may be foreseen:

(i) the introduction of efficient systems of information, directed towards parents and other partners in educational activities, about school life objectives and the outcomes of educational action. Providing clear information should be considered as a priority in all policies intended to stimulate partnership in education; and to encourage community resource mobilization;

(ii) the implementation of arrangements for participation in school life by families and other partners, such as parents' associations and councils, students' councils, support committees, tripartite councils (government, parents, enterprises) in vocational training school etc.;

(iii) the opening up of the school to society in parallel with the opening of social institutions to the schools. Co-operation between schools and businesses, the media and sports, and religious and cultural organisations, as well as other NGOs, should be encouraged in order to conduct training courses and other educational activities.

Recommendation No. 6

New Information and Communication Technologies: Serving to Improve the Quality of Education for All

1. The new information and communication technologies represent one of the key elements in a changing world. The report of the International Commission on Education for the Twenty-First Century has clearly demonstrated the implications resulting from the new technologies: by abolishing distance, they are instrumental in shaping the societies of tomorrow which, because of those technologies, will have nothing in common with any model from the past. The most accurate, up-to-date information can be made available to anyone, anywhere in the world. Let us not forget, however, that a very large underprivileged population remains excluded from these developments'.

(*i*) Furthermore, it should be borne in mind that the computerization of education is one of the most important means of achieving a new educational paradigm within which there is a shift of emphasis away from the more pragmatic objectives of narrow specialization and towards the acquisition of basic interdisciplinary knowledge. This new paradigm should considerably enhance the social value of education by renewing the potential of the content of education.

2. Panacea and threat are the two most polarized terms characterizing the debate on new information technologies and education. These two attitudes are based on a failure to appreciate the real educational potential of the new technologies and the most appropriate ways of using them. As a consequence, the educational system should learn to master them in order to avoid any technological, cultural and economic subjugation, as well as any marginalization of the school compared to other sectors.

3. In this situation, decisions about the application of new information technologies and their use in education should be taken with the objective of improving the quality of education for all and of enabling teachers to carry out their role of guide and advocate of learning among pupils.

4. On this basis, the measures to be adopted could deal with the following aspects:

(*i*) not limiting the application of new information technologies exclusively to the learning process. The use of these technologies in the administration and management of the school and the local community could save time for and improve the performance of teachers and other educational staff and allow them to devote themselves more to overcoming pupils' learning problems;

(*ii*) giving teachers, in the context of their pre-service education and training and career-long professional development, the opportunity not only of mastering the new information technologies for teaching purposes, in conjunction with other educational technologies, but also of contributing to the development of educational software and methodology. Special attention should be paid to distance education in the professionalization of teachers;

(iii) using new technologies to encourage communication, networks and exchange programmes among teachers, pupils and schools, at both national and international levels;

(iv) introducing ways of using new technologies based on the idea of technological resource centres available to all and allocating sufficient public funds to them. Harnessing the potential of these technologies in order to create easily accessible services which are designed to help and advice teachers in their daily work;

(v) encouraging and assisting the least developed countries to acquire and efficiently use the new information technologies in their education systems;

(vi) strengthening joint efforts among governments, educational authorities, teachers and teachers' organisations, businesses and industry to ensure the availability of adequate new information technologies at all levels of education;

(vii) developing research and information exchange on the impact, role and limitations of the new information and communication technologies in education.

Recommendation No. 7

Professionalization as a Strategy for Improving the Status and Working Conditions of Teachers

1. Even though the ICE is not the appropriate forum to analyse the working conditions of teachers, it is however evident that working conditions cannot be separated from policies on strengthening the role of teachers in a changing world.

Concern about the decline in the status of teachers is encountered frequently.

2. Although national and regional situations are highly diverse, improving the status of teachers often appears as a necessary condition for strengthening their role. But this improvement cannot be the outcome of a single measure or a single factor. On this subject, improving the material circumstances of teachers, particularly their salaries and other social benefits, is a necessary but insufficient condition for improving their status; it is the whole complex of educational issues that must be improved. In an integrated policy to improve the status of teachers, professionalization represents the most promising strategy in the medium and long terms. Beyond the recommendations made about their recruitment, their training, their participation in management and their autonomy in taking educational decisions, improving the status of teachers could be carried out along the following lines:

(i) promoting teacher professionalism, notably by the implementation of high levels of initial teacher education and career long professional development, the creation of diversified career structures underpinned by appropriate appraisal systems and improvements in the material and social status of teachers;

(ii) providing the necessary resources to ensure teacher training at the level of higher education;

(iii) implementing systematic strategies for drawing attention through the media to innovations and successful experiments carried out by teachers and groups of teachers;

(iv) exploiting pedagogical research effectively and making relevant use of existing information, in both the teaching and learning process and in the decision-making process;

(v) establishing performance incentives for teachers. These incentives need not be limited to monetary incentives

but could include opportunities for advanced training, formal recognition and career opportunities;

(vi) establishing a balance between the rights and responsibilities of teachers, as envisioned by the ILO/ UNESCO Recommendation concerning the Status of Teachers.

Recommendation No. 8

Solidarity with Teachers Working in Difficult Situations

1. Teachers in numerous countries are faced with the problem of teaching particular population groups (destitute people, marginalized groups, refugees, migrants, street children, delinquents, women from some traditional societies, etc.) or working under particularly difficult conditions (remote, mountainous or rural regions, multigrade or overpopulated classes, etc.). Armed conflicts, often crossing international borders, represent a particularly worrying situation. Children are always the victims who suffer most from conflicts and who will be affected by the psychological and moral consequences throughout their lives. Whatever the situation, whether it is a question of special population groups, remote regions or areas affected by armed conflict, an integrated and urgent strategy is needed to confront in practice specific educational situations. Despite their variety in size and type, all of these situations require of teachers, more than in any other circumstances, the mobilization of their emotional and psychological capacities and their various skills, in short true polyvalence. Yet, as has been observed, little or no time is devoted to the preparation of teachers to live and work in difficult situations.

2. Under such circumstances, the school and the teachers need, first of all moral and material support and—in the case of armed conflicts or natural catastrophes expressions of solidarity from the national and international communities, as well as rapid aid and intervention.

3. As a result, the following actions, modified for each particular case, could be foreseen:

(i) encouraging teachers originating from difficult areas and those motivated to work in such areas by organising pre-service and in-service training in these very places, backed up by a professional and psychological support network;

(ii) during the training of teachers expected to work in such situations, envisaging a further specialization, such as training as educational therapists, school psychologists or rehabilitation teachers. It would also seem desirable to reinforce preparation for the art of communication, negotiation and conflict resolution during their training;

(iii) backing up teachers and educators with support services, particularly by specialists in educational and vocational guidance and in educational psychology. This assistance could be provided, for example, by mobile advisory teams of specialists;

(iv) with a view to ensuring the recruitment of experienced and motivated educational teams, implementing incentive measures including, for example, allowances, advantages, an appropriate system of promotion and the possibility of transfer to calmer regions after a certain number of years of service in difficult situations or zones;

(v) ensuring the security of educational staff;

(vi) strengthening links and co-operation between teachers and the local community and, above all, with families and parents' associations;

(vii) developing all forms of national, regional and international solidarity with teachers who are working under difficult conditions, both from the material and from the technical and moral points of view.

Recommendation No. 9

Regional and International Co-operation: An Instrument to Promote Teacher Mobility and Competence

1. Participants in all the regional meetings expressed the opinion that strengthening the roles of teachers and their

in-service professional training requires joint efforts at the national, regional and international levels. This co-operation could be useful in supporting measures undertaken at the national level.

2. Member States are invited to enhance the role of teachers' competence through strengthening international co-operation in the following fields of actions:

(i) the development, mainly at the regional level, of networks of information centres, teacher training and educational research institutions, to facilitate the exchange of experiences, information and comparative research results concerning educational innovations and teacher education;

(ii) 'encouraging in-service training courses, study visits and exchange opportunities for teachers abroad, as well as partnerships between schools, teacher training institutions, and educational research institutes in different countries;

(iii) strengthening technical and financial assistance for the least developed countries in the field of education, particularly with the objective of improving educational materials and means, and developing pre-service and in-service teacher education;

(iv) seeking specific possibilities for improving the status of teachers in the least developed and the most indebted countries, for instance by reducing their debts by sums corresponding to the increasing for this purpose in their budgets;

(v) promoting and expanding the participation of schools in the Associated Schools Project (ASP) of UNESCO;

(vi) marking the celebration of International Teachers' Day—5 October—as a special opportunity to congratulate teachers, to make known their experiences and thus to contribute to improving the profession's social value and the teachers' image;

(vii) UNESCO and its partners should be invited to:

— strengthen their assistance to Member States in order to develop their national systems of educational information, innovation and their teacher training systems, having recourse particularly to the possibilities offered by new technologies and the existing regional and sub-regional networks;

— make Member States aware of the outcomes of comparative studies concerning innovations in teachers training and in ways of employing new information and communication technologies in education;

— assist Member States in applying the ILO/UNESCO Recommendation concerning the Status of Teachers (1966).

III. DRAFT DECLARATION OF THE 45TH SESSION OF THE INTERNATIONAL CONFERENCE ON EDUCATION

We, the Ministers of Education, meeting at the forty fifth session of the International Conference on Education.

Concerned: about the need to develop understanding and new, more active and just forms of solidarity between the individuals peoples and generations;

Taking Into Account: the profound social, economic, political and cultural changes that our societies are undergoing, and the highly precarious situation prevailing in many countries with regard to poverty, health and nutrition, which makes the development, adaptation and transformation of education systems an urgent priority;

Recognizing: the importance that the contribution of teachers brings to the renewal of education through their ideas, methods and practices;

Convinced: that teachers are key actors in educational change which must take place as much within the school and classroom at levels and in all types, and through all channels of schooling, as within the education system as a whole;

Aware: that the accelerated pace of change means that teachers must be capable not only of helping and guiding learners to assimilate knowledge but also to become aware of their identify and be tolerant, open to others and to other cultures, capable to pursuing their learning throughout life, so enabling them to face the future with confidence;

Aware: that the spread of new technologies is bound to change the conditions of the teaching profession and the nature of the teacher-learner relationship;

Noting: the terms of existing international conventions which are applicable to teachers, and in particular of instruments concerned with basic human rights such as the Freedom of Association and Protection of the Right to Organise Convention, 1948, the Right to Organise and Collective Bargaining Convention, 1949, the Equal Remuneration Convention, 1951, adopted by the General Conference of the International Labour Organisation, and the Convention Against Discrimination in Education, 1960, adopted by the General Conference of the United Educational Nations Scientific and Cultural Organisation;

Recalling: the 1966 ILO/UNESCO Recommendation concerning the Status of Teachers and the reports of the joint ILO/UNESCO Committee of Experts on its application, Recommendation No. 69 adopted in 1975 by the thirty-fifth session of the International Conference on Education on the changing role of the teacher and its influence on preparation for the profession and on in-service training, as well as the Declaration of the forty-fourth session of the ICE (1994), which called for priority to be given to the training of educational personnel oriented 'notably towards professional ethics civic and moral education, cultural diversity, national codes and internationally recognized standards of human rights and fundamental freedoms';

Declare Ourselves Determined

1. to ensure the active participation of teachers and all educational partners in the processes of changing education systems according to the forms of consultation and co-ordination appropriate to the socio-economic, political and cultural contexts of their societies;
2. to develop and implement integrated policies designed to recruit and retain in the teaching profession motivated and able individuals of both genders; to reform pre-service and

in-service education in order that they shall serve the new challenges facing education; to adopt measures encouraging educational innovations; to strengthen professional autonomy and sense of responsibility of teachers; and to improve their status and their working conditions;

3. to place these integrated policies within the framework of strategies intended to ensure relevance of and equity of access to high-quality education, to promote lifelong learning and to make the school one of the main tools in achieving social cohesion and in training for democratic values and the culture of peace;

4. to develop, at the national, regional and international levels, all forms of support, particularly with teachers who are working in difficult situations, such as those of extreme poverty, armed conflict, social exclusion or in remote areas;

5. to call upon all the partners, such as teachers and their associations, learners themselves, moral and spiritual authorities, families, businesses, the media, intellectuals, artists and scientists to commit themselves to the development of a school envisaged as an active centre for learning and moral, spiritual, civic and vocational education, to be continually adapted to a changing world;

6. to be inspired in our action by the Recommendations accompanying this Declaration that we are adopting in Geneva on 5 October, 1996 International Teachers' Day.

Courtesy: UNESCO, UNESCO-IBE and IBE Director Prof. Juan Carlos Tedesco.

Bibliography

Bhaskara Rao, Digumarti (1994). *Scientific Aptitude*. New Delhi: Ashish Publishing House. pp: 100. Rs. 100. ISBN 81-7024-658-X.

Bhaskara Rao, Digumarti (1995). *Animal Kingdom*. New Delhi: Discovery Publishing House. pp: 135. Rs. 200. ISBN 81-7141-274-2.

Bhaskara Rao, Digumarti (1995). *Batracology*. New Delhi: Discovery Publishing House. pp: 174. Rs. 250 ISBN 81-7141-279-3.

Bhaskara Rao, Digumarti (1996). *Scientific Attitude vis-a-vis Scientific Aptitude*. New Delhi: Discovery Publishing House. pp: 143 Rs. 275. ISBN 81-7141-308-0.

Bhaskara Rao, Digumarti, ed. (1996). *Encyclopaedia of Education For All*, 5 vols. New Delhi: APH Publishing Corporation. pp: 1460. Rs. 3000. ISBN 81-7024-759-4. (set).

Vol. I — Education For All: The World Conference pp: 440. ISBN 81-7024-760-8.

Vol. II — Education For All: The EPA—9 Summit. pp: 340. ISBN 81-7024-761-6.

Vol. III — Education For All: Quality Education For All. pp: 250. ISBN 81-7024-762-4.

Vol. IV — Education For All: Planning and Monitoring. pp: 170. ISBN 81-7024-763-2.

Vol. V — Education For All: The Indian Scenario. pp: 260. ISBN 81-7024-764-0.

Bhaskara Rao, Digumarti, ed. (1996). *Global Perceptions on Peace Education*, 3 vols. New Delhi: Discovery Publishing House. pp: 980 Rs. 1800. ISBN 81-7141-319-6.

Bhaskara Rao, Digumarti, ed. (1996). *National Policy on Education*, 2 Vols. New Delhi: Anmol Publications Pvt. Ltd. pp: 710. Rs. 1000. ISBN 81-7488-323-1.

Bhaskara Rao, Digumarti, ed. (1997). *Care the Child*. 2 Vols. New Delhi: Discovery Publishing House. pp: 616. Rs. 1000. ISBN 81-7141-394-3.

Bhaskara Rao, Digumarti, ed. (1997). *Education for the 21st Century*. New Delhi: Discovery Publishing House. pp: 288. Rs. 500. ISBN 81-7141-389-7.

Bhaskara Rao, Digumarti, ed. (1997). *Reflections on Scientific Attitude*. New Delhi: Discovery Publishing House. pp: 310. Rs. 500. ISBN 81-7141-328-5.

Bhaskara Rao, Digumarti (1997). *Scientific Attitude*. New Delhi: Discovery Publishing House. pp: 120. Rs. 225. ISBN 81-7141-381-1.

Bhaskara Rao, Digumarti, ed. (1997). *Success Story of a Primary Education Project*. New Delhi: APH Publishing Corporation. pp: 260. Rs. 400. ISBN 81-7024-850-7.

Bhaskara Rao, Digumarti, ed. (1997) *World Food Summit*. New Delhi: Discovery Publishing House. pp: 153. Rs. 300. ISBN 81-7141-386-2.

Bhaskara Rao, Digumarti, ed. (1998). *Adolescence Education*. New Delhi: Discovery Publishing House. pp: 238. Rs. 350. ISBN 81-7141-432-X.

Bhaskara Rao, Digumarti, ed. (1998). *Community and School Nutrition Education*. New Delhi: Discovery Publishing House. pp: 425. Rs. 650. ISBN 81-7141-435-4.

Bhaskara Rao, Digumarti, ed. (1998). *District Primary Education Programme*. New Delhi: Discovery Publishing House. pp: 506. Rs. 650. ISBN 81-7141-396-X.

Bhaskara Rao, Digumarti, ed. (1998). *Earth Summit*, 2 Vols. New Delhi: Discovery Publishing House. pp: 930. Rs. 1500. ISBN 81-7141-435-4.

Bhaskara Rao, Digumarti. ed. (1998). *National Policy on Education: Towards an Enlightened and Humane Society*. New Delhi: Discovery Publishing House. pp: 542. Rs. 860. ISBN 81-7141-426-5.

Bhaskara Rao, Digumarti, ed. (1998). *Reforming School Education*. New Delhi: Discovery Publishing House. pp: 575. Rs. 750. ISBN 81-7141-403-6.

Bhaskara Rao, Digumarti, ed. (1998). *Teacher Education in India*. New Delhi: Discovery Publishing House. pp: 424. Rs. 600. ISBN 81-7141-406-0.

Bhaskara Rao, Digumarti, ed. (1998). *World Summit for Social Development.* New Delhi: Discovery Publishing House. pp: 278. Rs. 450. ISBN 81-7141-420-6.

Bhaskara Rao, Digumarti, ed. (2000). *Education For All: Achieving the Goal.* 3 vols. New Delhi: APH Publishing Corporation. pp: 830. Rs. 2000. ISBN 81-7648-152-1.

Vol. I The Global Consensus. pp: 285. ISBN 81-7648-153-X.

Vol. II Mid-Decade Review Reports of Regional Seminars. pp: 198. ISBN 81-7648-154-8.

Vol. III Issues and Trends. pp: 346. ISBN 81-7648-155-6.

Bhaskara Rao, Digumarti, ed. (2000). *International Encyclopaedia of AIDS,* 11 Vols. in 13 parts. New Delhi: Discovery Publishing House. pp: 3676. Rs. 7500. ISBN 81-7141-465-6 (set).

Vol. 1 Introduction to HIV/AIDS. pp: 246. Rs. 500. ISBN 81-7141-523-7.

Vol. 2 HIV/AIDS—Issues and Challenges, 2 parts. pp: 805. Rs. 1700. ISBN 81-7141-524-5.

Vol. 3 HIV/AIDS—Socio Economic Realities. pp: 436. Rs. 900. ISBN 81-7141-525-3.

Vol. 4 HIV/AIDS Law Ethics and Human Rights, 2 parts. pp: 859. Rs. 1800. ISBN 81-7141-526-1.

Vol. 5 AIDS and NGOs. pp: 215. Rs. 450 ISBN 81-7141-527-X.

Vol. 6 Aids and Home Care pp: 183. Rs. 400 ISBN 81-7141-528-8.

Vol. 7 STD Case Management pp: 223. Rs. 475 ISBN 81-7141-529-6.

Vol. 8 HIV Prevention and Care—Teaching Modules for Nurses and Midwives. pp: 125. Rs. 275. ISBN 81-7141-530-X.

Vol. 9 HIV/AIDS Prevention Education for Educational Institutions. pp: 75. Rs. 150. ISBN 81-7141-531-8.

Vol. 10 Instructional Modules for AIDS Education. pp: 111. Rs. 250. ISBN 81-7141-532-6.

Vol. 11 School Health Education to Prevent AIDS and STD—A package for curriculum planners. pp: 298. Rs. 600. ISBN 81-7141-533-4.

Bhaskara Rao, Digumarti, ed. (2000). *International Encyclopaedia of Science and Technology Education.* 11 Volumes. New Delhi: Discovery Publishing House. pp: 4892. Rs. 8500. ISBN 81-7141-548-2 (set).

Vol. 1 Science and Technology Education. pp: 557. Rs. 975 ISBN 81-7141-568-7.

Vol. 2 Science Education in Developing Countries. pp: 334. Rs. 600 ISBN 81-7141-570-9.

Vol. 3 Organisational Structure of Science. pp: 334. Rs. 600. ISBN 81-7141-570-9.

Vol. 4 Science Education in Asia and the Pacific. pp: 429. Rs. 750 ISBN 81-7141-571-7.

Vol. 5 Science and Technology Education For All. pp: 464. Rs. 800 ISBN 81-7141-572-5.

Vol. 6 Values, Ethics, Talent and Girls in Science and Technology Education. pp: 463. Rs. 800 ISBN 81-7141-573-3.

Vol. 7 Popularization of Science and Technology Education. pp. 334. Rs. 600. ISBN 81-7141-574-1.

Vol. 8 Scientific, Power and Society. pp: 357. Rs. 625 ISBN 81-7141-575-X.

Vol. 9 Information Technology. pp: 442. Rs. 775. ISBN 81-7141-576-8.

Vol. 10 Teacher Training in Science and Technology Education. pp: 536. Rs. 975. ISBN 81-7141-577-6.

Vol. 11 Science, Technology and Society: A Curriculum Framework. pp: 642. Rs. 1000. ISBN 81-7141-578-4.

Bhaskara Rao, Digumarti, ed. (2001). *Distance Education in Different Countries*. New Delhi: APH Publishing Corporation. pp: 574. Rs. 1500. ISBN 81-7648-229-3.

Bhaskara Rao, Digumarti, ed. (2001). *Decentralised Management of Education (Management of Education in Panchayati Raj and Municipal Bodies)*. New Delhi: Discovery Publishing House. pp: 116. Rs. 250. ISBN 81-7141-617-9.

Bhaskara Rao, Digumarti, ed. (2001). *Electrochemistry for Environmental Protection*. New Delhi: Discovery Publishing House. pp: 208. Rs. 400. ISBN 81-7141-619-5.

Bhaskara Rao, Digumarti, ed. (2001). *Global Educational Studies*. New Delhi: Discovery Publishing House. pp: 145. Rs. 300. ISBN 81-7141-616-0.

Bhaskara Rao, Digumarti, ed. (2001) *Global Synthesis of Educational Assessment*. New Delhi: Discovery Publishing House. pp: 152. Rs. 300. ISBN 81-7141-613-6.

Bhaskara Rao. Digumarti, ed. (2001). *International Encyclopaedia of Human Rights*. 7 Volumes in 13 parts. New Delhi. Discovery Publishing House. pp: 6500 (Royal size). Rs. 22000. ISBN 81-7141-567-9 (set).

Vol. 1 International Instruments of Human Rights. 2 parts Rs. 3500. ISBN 81-7141-595-4.

Vol. 2 Regional Instruments of Human Rights. Rs. 1500 ISBN 81-7141-604-7.

Vol. 3 Human Rights and the United Nations, 2 parts. Rs. 2800. ISBN 81-7141-605-5.

Vol. 4 Fact Files of Human Rights, 2 parts. Rs. 3000. ISBN 81-7141-606-3.

Vol. 5 Study Stories of Human Rights, 3 parts. Rs. 5200. ISBN 81-7141-607-1.

Vol. 6 International Meetings on Human Rights, 2 parts. Rs. 3800. ISBN 81-7141-608-X.

Vol. 7 Professional Training in Human Rights. Rs. 2200. ISBN 81-7141-609-8.

Bhaskara Rao, Digumarti, ed. (2001). *Jomtein Decade of Education*. New Delhi: Discovery Publishing House. pp: 106. Rs. 225. ISBN 81-7141-618-7.

Bhaskara Rao, Digumarti, ed. (2001). *Nuclear Materials: Issues and Concerns*, 2 Vols. New Delhi: Discovery Publishing House. pp: 1100. Rs. 2200. ISBN 81-7141-611-X.

Bhaskara Rao, Digumarti, ed. (2001). *World Conference on Education for All*. New Delhi: APH Publishing Corporation. pp: 380. Rs. 995. ISBN 81-7648-274-9.

Bhaskara Rao, Digumarti, ed. (2001). *World Conference on Higher Education*. New Delhi: Discovery Publishing House. pp: 306. Rs. 600. ISBN 81-7141-610-1.

Bhaskara Rao, Digumarti, ed. (2001). *World Conference on Science*. New Delhi: Discovery Publishing House. pp: 85. Rs. 200. ISBN 81-7141-612-8.

Bhaskara Rao, Digumarti, C.A.P. Swamy and B.S.V. Dutt (1997). *Self Evaluation in Student Teaching*. New Delhi: Discovery Publishing House. pp: 762. Rs. 150. ISBN 81-7141-374-9.

Bhaskara Rao, Digumarti, C. Sridevi and K. Vijaya (1995). *Achievement in Social Studies*. New Delhi: Discovery Publishing House. pp: 102. Rs. 150. ISBN 81-7141-281-5.

Bhaskara Rao, Digumarti and Digumarti Pushpa Latha (1994). *Achievement in Biology*. New Delhi: Discovery Publishing House. pp: 102. Rs. 125. ISBN 81-7141-264-5.

Bhaskara Rao. Digumarti and Digumarti Pushpa Latha (1995). *Achievement in English*. New Delhi: Discovery Publishing House. pp: 214. Rs. 275. ISBN 81-7141-283-1.

Bhaskara Rao, Digumarti and Digumarti Pushpa Latha (1995). *Achievement in Science*. New Delhi: Discovery Publishing House. pp: 159. Rs. 225. ISBN 81-7141-280-7.

Bhaskara Rao, Digumarti and Digumarti Pushpa Latha (1995). *Achievement in Mathematics*. New Delhi: Discovery Publishing House. pp: 125. Rs. 175. ISBN 81-7141-278-5.

Bhaskara Rao, Digumarti and Digumarti Pushpa Latha, eds. (1998). *International Encyclopaedia of Women*, 5 Vols. New Delhi: Discovery Publishing House. pp: 2172. Rs. 4000. ISBN 81-7141-410-9.

Vol. 1 Status of World's Women pp: 427. Rs. 750. ISBN 81-7141-494-X.

Vol. 2 Women, Education and Empowerment. pp: 467. Rs. 875. ISBN 81-7141-498-2.

Vol. 3 Women Challenges and Advancement. pp: 354. Rs. 650. ISBN 81-7141-497-4.

Vol. 4 Women and Family Health. pp: 470. Rs. 875. ISBN 81-7141-497-4.

Vol. 5 Women and International Action. pp: 453. Rs. 850. ISBN 81-7141-498-2.

Bhaskara Rao, Digumarti, Digumarti Pushpa Latha and Digumarti Harshitha, eds. (2001). *Biological Warfare*. New Delhi: Discovery Publishing House. pp: 422. Rs. 800. ISBN 81-7141-597-0.

Bhaskara Rao, Digumarti, Digumarti Pushpa Latha and Digumarti Harshitha, eds. (2001). *Women as Educators*. New Delhi: Discovery Publishing House. pp: 112. Rs. 200. ISBN 81-7141-602-0.

Bhaskara Rao, Digumarti and Digumarti Harshitha (2000). *Education in India*. New Delhi: APH Publishing Corporation. pp: 280. Rs. 700. ISBN 81-7648-207-2.

Bhaskara Rao, Digumarti, and Digumarti Harshitha eds. (2001). *Assessing Learning Achievement*. New Delhi: Discovery Publishing House. pp: 128. Rs. 225. ISBN 81-7141-601-2.

Bhaskara Rao, Digumarti and Digumarti Harshita, eds. (2001). *Energy Security*. New Delhi: Discovery Publishing House. pp: 564. Rs. 1000. ISBN 81-7141-598-9.

Bhaskara Rao, Digumarti, D. Harshitha and K.R.S.S. Rao. eds. (1999). *Advanced Biotechnology*. New Delhi: Discovery Publishing House. pp: 335. Rs. 550. ISBN 81-7141-516-4.

Bhaskara Rao, Digumarti and K.R.S. Sambasiva Rao, eds. (1996). *Current Trends in Indian Education*. New Delhi: Discovery Publishing House. pp: 234. Rs. 400. ISBN 81-7141-311-0.

Bhaskara Rao, Digumarti and K. Vijaya (1995). *A Text Book Evaluation*. Ambala Cantt: The Associated Publishers. pp: 100. Rs. 160.

Bhaskara Rao, Digumarti, V.V. Rao, V.V. Lakshmi and V.V. Krishna, eds. (2000). *Status and Advancement of Women*. New Delhi: APH Publishing Corporation. pp: 570. Rs. 1100. ISBN 81-7648-169-6.

Bhagya Lakshmi, Lingineni and Digumarti Bhaskara Rao, ed. (2000). *Reading and Comprehension*. New Delhi: Discovery Publishing House. pp: 108. Rs. 175. ISBN 81-7141-543-1.

Bhuvaneswara Lakshmi, G. and Digumarti Bhaskara Rao, ed. (2000). *Attitude Towards Science*. New Delhi: Discovery Publishing House. pp: 128. Rs. 250. ISBN 81-7141-541-6.

Devraj, T.A.S. and Digumarti Bhaskara Rao, ed. (1997). *Trace Analysis of Uranium and Thorum*. New Delhi: Discovery Publishing House. pp: 195. Rs. 350. ISBN 81-7141-375-7.

Durgani Rani, K and Digumarti Bhaskara Rao, ed. (2000). *Educational Aspirations and Scientific Attitudes*. New Delhi: Discovery Publishing House. pp: 130. Rs. 250. ISBN 81-7141-555-55.

Dutt, B.S.V. and Digumarti Bhaskara Rao (2001). *Empowering Primary Teachers*. New Delhi: Discovery Publishing House. pp. 283. Rs. 475. ISBN 81-7141-615-2.

Ediger, Marlow and Digumarti Bhaskara Rao (1996). *Science Curriculum*. New Delhi: Discovery Publishing House. pp: 309. Rs. 450. ISBN 81-7141-321-8.

Ediger, Marlow and Digumarti Bhaskara Rao (2000). *Teaching Mathematics Successfully*. New Delhi: Discovery Publishing House. pp: 279. Rs. Rs. 525. ISBN 81-7141-552-0.

Ediger, Marlow and Digumarti Bhaskara Rao (2000). *Teaching Reading Successfully*. New Delhi. New Delhi: Discovery Publishing House. pp: 386. Rs. 750. ISBN 81-7141-556-3.

Ediger Marlow and Digumarti Bhaskara Rao (2001). *Teaching Science Successfully*. New Delhi: Discovery Publishing House. pp: 320. Rs. 600. ISBN 81-7141-600-4.

Ediger. Marlow and Digumarti Bhaskara Rao (2001). *Teaching Social Studies Successfully*. New Delhi: Discovery Publishing House. pp: 296. Rs. 575. ISBN 81-7141-596-2.

Jayasree. Kandi and Digumarti Bhaskara Rao. ed. (1999). *Correlates of Socialisation*. New Delhi: Discovery Publishing House. pp: 160. Rs. 375. ISBN 81-7141-517-2.

John Babu. Ch., T.J.R. Prasad, G.M. Madhukar and Digumarti Bhaskara Rao, eds. (2001). *Problem Solving in Mathematics*. New Delhi: APH Publishing Corporation. pp: 125. Rs. 250. ISBN 81-7648-273-0.

Marja, Talvi and Digumarti Bhaskara Rao, eds. (1996). *Educational Leadership and Social Changes*. New Delhi: Discovery Publishing House. pp: 236. Rs. 400. ISBN 8-7141-320-X.

Prabhakaram, K.S. and Digumarti Bhaskara Rao, ed. (1998). *Concept Attainment Model in Mathematics Teaching*. New Delhi: Discovery Publishing House. pp: 122. Rs. 200. ISBN 81-7141-424-9.

Prasanth Kumar, J. and Digumarti Bhaskara Rao, ed. (1998). *Effectiveness of Distance Education System*. New Delhi: Discovery Publishing. pp: 152. Rs. 275. ISBN 81-7141-437-0.

Prasanth Kumar, J., and Digumarti Bhaskara Rao and G. Sundara Rao, eds. (2000). *Open University Student Support Services*. New Delhi: Discovery Publishing House. pp: 100. Rs. 200. ISBN 81-7141-550-4.

Rama Krishnaiah, D and Digumarti Bhaskara Rao, ed. (1998). *Job Satisfaction of College Teachers*. New Delhi: Discovery Publishing House. pp: 251. Rs. 400. ISBN 81-7141-438-9.

Ramesh, Ganta and Digumarti Bhaskara Rao, eds. (1998). *Environmental Education: Problems and Prospects*. New Delhi: Discovery Publishing House. pp: 324. Rs. 525. ISBN 81-7141-423-0.

Rathaiah, L. and Digumarti Bhaskara Rao, eds. (1997). *International Innovations in Education*. New Delhi: Discovery Publishing House. pp: 514. Rs. 750. ISBN 81-7141-359-5.

Rathaiah, Lavu, Digumarti Bhaskara Rao and Paturi Koteswara Rao. (1997). *Achievement Correlates*. New Delhi: Discovery Publishing House. pp: 116. Rs. 225. ISBN 81-7141-385-4.

Sanjeeva Rao, P.C. and Digumarti Bhaskara Rao. ed. (1996). *A Text Book of Geology*. New Delhi: Discovery Publishing House. pp: 320. Rs. 525 ISBN 81-7141-313-7.

Satya Narayana, V and Digumarti Bhaskara Rao, ed. (2001). *Physical Education, Social Attitudes and Leadership Qualities.* New Delhi: Discovery Publishing House. pp: 296. Rs. 575. ISBN 81-7141-593-8.

Srinivasulu Reddy, M., K.R.S. Sambasiva Rao and Digumarti Bhaskara Rao, ed. (1999). *A Text Book of Agriculture.* New Delhi: Discovery Publishing House. pp: 296. Rs. 525. ISBN 81-7141-482-6.

Vanaja, M. and Digumarti Bhaskara Rao, ed. (1999). *Inquiry Training Model.* New Delhi: Discovery Publishing House. pp: 189. Rs. 325. ISBN 81-7141-515-6.

Veena Kumari, Balusu and Digumarti Bhaskara Rao (1996). *Operation Black Board.* New Delhi: APH Publishing Corporation. pp: 140. Rs. 200. ISBN 81 7024-711-X.

Veena Kumari, B. and Digumarti Bhaskara Rao, ed. (2000). *Psycho Social Correlates of Achievement.* New Delhi: Discovery Publishing House. pp: 136. Rs. 300. ISBN 81-7141-547-4.

Venkata Rao, P and Digumarti Bhaskara Rao (1989). *A Text Book of Zoology—Junior Intermediate.* Guntur: Vignan Publishers. pp: 370. Rs. 57.

Venkata Rao, P. and Digumarti Bhaskara Rao (1989). *A Text Book of Zoology—Senior Intermediate.* Guntur: Vignan Publishers. pp: 480. Rs. 68.

Venugopala Rao, K and Digumarti Bhaskara Rao, ed. (2000). *Teacher Morale in Secondary Schools.* New Delhi: Discovery Publishing House. pp: 300. Rs. 575. ISBN 81-7141-551-2.

Vidya, C and Digumarti Bhaskara Rao, ed. (1996). *A Text Book of Nutrition.* New Delhi: Discovery Publishing House. pp: 438. Rs. 650. ISBN 81-7141-309-9.

Vijaya Bharathi, D. and Digumarti Bhaskara Rao, ed. (2000). *Educational Philosophies of Swami Vivekanand and John Dewey.* New Delhi: APH Publishing Corporation. pp: 200. Rs. 500. ISBN 81-7648-202-1.

Bhaskara Rao, Digumarti. (1986). *Dhrushya Sravana Bodhanapakaranalu* (Audio Visual Teaching Aids). Guntur: Nagarjuna Publishers.

Bhaskara Rao, Digumarti (1993). *Jeevasashtra Bodhana* (Teaching of Biology). Guntur: Nagarjuna Publishers.

Bhaskara Rao, Digumarti (1995). *Vignanasasthra Bodhana.* (Teaching of Science). Guntur: Nagarjuna Publishers.

Bhaskara Rao, Digumarti (1997). *Vidya Manovignana Sashtram.* (Educational Psychology). Guntur: Creative Press. pp. 434. Rs. 79.

Bhaskara Rao, Digumarti (1998). *DSC Study Material*. Guntur: Nagarjuna Publishers.

Bhaskara Rao, Digumarti (1998). *Upadhyayudu Vidya* (Teacher and Education). Guntur: Nagarjuna Publishers.

Bhaskara Rao, Digumarti (1998). *Vidya Dhrukpadhalu*. (Perspectives of Education). Guntur: Nagarjuna Publishers.

Bhaskara Rao, Digumarti (1999). *EdCET Teaching Aptitude*. Guntur: Nagarjuna Publishers.

Bhaskara Rao, Digumarti (2001). *Bharata Samajamulo Upadhayayudu Vidya*. (Teacher and Education in Emerging Indian Society). Guntur: Nagarjuna Publishers. pp: 256. Rs. 59.

Bhaskara Rao, Digumarti (2001). *Bhoutika Sastra Bodhana Padhatulu* (Methods of Teaching Physical Science). Guntur: Nagarjuna Publishers. pp: 324. Rs. 77.

Bhaskara Rao, Digumarti (2001). *Jeeva Sastra Bodhana Padhatulu* (Methods of Teaching Biological Science). Guntur: Nagarjuna Publishers. pp: 224. Rs. 59.

Bhaskara Rao, Digumarti (2001). *Vidya Manovignana Sastram* (Educational Psychology). Guntur: Nagarjuna Publishers. pp: 344. Rs. 77.